Essential Skills
for Papua New Guinea

Spelling

GRADE 3

Peter Durkin

OXFORD

Oxford University Press is a department of the University of Oxford.

It furthers the University's objective of excellence in research, scholarship, and education by publishing worldwide. Oxford is a registered trademark of Oxford University Press in the UK and in certain other countries.

Published in Australia by
Oxford University Press
253 Normanby Road, South Melbourne, Victoria 3205, Australia

First published 2013

ISBN 978 0 195518412

Edited by Emma Short
Cover design by Sarah Hazell
Text design by Sarah Hazell
Typeset by Sarah Hazell
Illustrations by Birdwing Group
Printed in China by Golden Cup Printing Co. Ltd

To the Student ›

This book will help you learn about spelling. You will learn:

The different sounds that letters can make, for example:

- 'd' as in drum
- 's' as in snake
- 'g' as in garden.

The letters and sounds that can be used to make words, for example:

- c + at = cat
- d + og = dog
- st + ing = sting
- cl + uck = cluck.

You will also learn some 'common words'.

They are important because you use them in your writing.
Some common words are difficult to sound out, so you need to practise spelling them every day.

Some examples of common words are:

- where → **Where** are you going?
- was → Kila **was** late for school today.
- said → "It's time for bed," **said** Mum.

Learning to spell can be a challenge but if you work at it, you will get better and better.
After you have finished each unit in this book, think about what you have learnt.
If anything is still a little confusing, ask your teacher for help.
And remember, you will learn to spell unknown or tricky words faster if you practise spelling these words every day.

LOOK, COVER, WRITE, CHECK

Practise your weekly Spelling List this way:

1. LOOK carefully at the word.
2. COVER the word.
3. WRITE the word from memory.
4. CHECK to see if your spelling is correct.

CONTENTS ›

Term 3

	Topic	Focus	Spelling Words	Word Knowledge
21	Words ending in '–ll'	'–ell', '–oll', '–ull' words	yes, you, will, good, food, well, smell, fill, roll, tell	Plural words
22	Words ending in '–rn'	'–arn', '–ern', '–orn', '–urn' words	going, house, into, little, here, worn, barn, fern, born, corn	Unusual plural words
23	Words ending in '–tch'	'–atch', '–etch', '–itch', '–otch', '–utch' words	make, made, morning, night, what, hatch, fetch, ditch, blotch, clutch	Verbs
24	Words ending in '–le'	'–ale', '–ile', '–ule', '–ole' words	looked, played, off, one, in, sale, file, stole, rule, pale	Verbs
25	'–ll', '–rn', '–tch', '–le' words	Revision		
26	Words ending in '–me'	'–ame', '–ime', '–ome' words	saw, tree, them, under, because, shame, home, flame, crime, name	Past tense verbs
27	Words ending in '–ke'	'–ake', '–ike', '–oke' words	very, where, name, after, said, like, smoke, bike, snake, wake	Irregular past tense verbs
28	Words ending in '–ce'	'–ace', '–ice' words	brother, sister, down, this, give, race, price, lace, twice, face	Present tense verbs
29	Words ending in '–ne'	'–ane', '–ine', '–one' words	quickly , quietly, play, people, was, cane, wine, bone, lane, line	Adverbs
30	'–me', '–ke', '–ce', '–ne' words	Revision		

Term 4

	Topic	Focus	Spelling Words	Word Knowledge
31	Words ending in '–de'	'–ade', '–ide', '–ode', '–ude' words	it's, I'm, home, has, don't, pride, made, code, rude, bride	Contractions
32	Words ending in '–te'	'–ate', '–ite' words	away, back, come, car, old, gate, kite, write, plate, state	Contractions
33	Words ending in '–y'	'–ay', '–oy' words	every, first, get, got, very, day, spray, boy, joy, pay	Opposites
34	Words ending in '–at'	'–eat', '–oat' words	over, one, put, some, fix, meat, cheat, boat, float, treat	Connecting words
35	'–de', '–te', '–y', '–at' words	Revision		
36	Words ending in '–rk'	'–ark', '–ork' words	door, two, three, four, five, park, spark, stork, pork, fork	Prefix 'un'
37	Words ending in '–rt'	'–art', '–irt', '–ort', '–urt' words	too, their, school, room, fun, skirt, smart, sport, start, port	Comparisons
38	Words ending in '–il'	'–ail', '–oil' words	our, kick, jumped, how, six, snail, oil, sail, soil, spoil	Compound words
39	Words ending in '–t'	'–eet', '–oot' words	where, water, two, your, seven, eight, scoot, feet, meet, sweet	Adjectives and nouns
40	'–rk', '–rt', '–il', '–t' words	Revision		

To the Teacher ›

About the **Essential Spelling Skills** series

The **Essential Spelling Skills** series is a sequential, developmental spelling program that will provide primary students in Grade 3 to 8 with strategies and skills to become independent spellers in English. Each book has been designed as a full year's spelling program consisting of 40 three-page units of work.

Learning to spell strategies

Good spellers use these strategies to help them become successful:

- **Phonological strategies** – how word and letter combinations sound.
- **Visual strategies** – how word and letter combinations look.
- **Morphemic strategies** – how words take different spellings when they change form (for example, church – churches).
- **Etymological strategies** – how words are spelt and where they come from (for example, aeroplane = 'aero' meaning air + 'plane' meaning a flat surface).
- **Inquiry strategies** – how to use learning tools such as a dictionary or thesaurus to spell difficult or unknown words.

These strategies are the basis for learning to spell at every level of this series. In the early levels – Grades 3, 4, and 5 – the emphasis is on visual and phonological strategies to allow children to develop a firm base on which to build more complex understandings of English spelling. In the upper levels – Grades 6, 7 and 8 – there is an increasing emphasis on developing morphemic knowledge and understanding English constructions.

A useful strategy to assist the students' learning, as well as provide the teacher with valuable guidance to students' progress, is the 'Have-A-Go-Card'. To make the simplest 'Have-A-Go-Card', divide a sheet of card or paper into three columns. The students have a go at spelling the word in the first two columns. They tick the spelling they think is correct and check this spelling with their teacher. The teacher confirms the correct spelling and writes it in the third column.

beter ✓	better	better
were	where ✓	where
brake ✓	break	break
realy	really ✓	really
wobling	wobbling ✓	wobbling

How to use the **Essential Spelling Skills** series

This spelling program consists of 40 units of work – ten units per term. Each unit consists of three pages of work including sufficient activities for a five-day spelling program. The first two pages in each unit concentrate on developing spelling strategies to tackle unknown words and the third page allows students to learn more about English, including grammar and writing skills. The units include written activities that are designed to show that spelling is not an isolated skill, but is essential for the development of literacy skills. An assessment program is built into each unit and is usually completed on the fifth day. This is designed to help the teacher test students' spelling knowledge on a regular basis.

Example unit – Term 2 Week 2

The following example shows how a unit of work can be broken down into a week's program using the five spelling strategies. It demonstrates how each unit contains one full week's work relating specifically to spelling, but also incorporates reading and writing.

Unit 12	Focus	Spelling strategy	Teacher preparation	Activities/tasks
Day 1	Words that end in '**–ick**', '**–ack**', '**–ock**' and '**–uck**'	Phonological	Make a chart with the Word List or write the Word List on the board. These '**–ck**' words need to be displayed for the whole week as this is the unit focus. Draw a large empty '**–ck**' truck on the board similar to the one in the student book.	**1.** As a class, read all the words on the Word List, pointing out the different phonetic sounds, for example: sick/sock, lick/luck, stick/stuck. **2.** Choose words from the Word List and ask students to use them (orally) in a complete sentence. **3.** Talk about activities 1 to 2 (orally) before students complete them in the student book. **4.** Students complete the Off the page activity to consolidate learning relating to '**–ck**' words.
Day 2		Phonological	Copy the '**Quick, Quick**' rhyme on a chart or on the board, making it large enough for students to read.	**1.** Reinforce point 1 from Day 1 above. **2.** Talk about activities 3 to 6 (orally) before you ask students to complete them. **3.** Complete the Rhyme time activity. Read the rhyme and have fun with the '**–ck**' words, before students complete the extension activity.
Day 3	There are ten spelling words – five common words and five '**–ck**' words.	Visual	Copy the ten spelling words on the board. Students learn these words by applying the stategy: **Look** – at the word **Cover** – the word **Write** – the word **Check** – the spelling	**1.** As a class, read the spelling words. Choose students to use these words (orally) in complete sentences. **2.** Play games with the spelling words to help the students memorise them. For example, ask students to close their eyes and attempt to spell a given word. **3.** Students copy the spelling words in their book. **4.** During the week, students need to practise spelling these words. Tell students that these words will be tested at the end of the week.
Day 4		Word knowledge (inquiry strategy)	Draw an empty noun box on the board.	**1.** Reinforce the purpose of a noun. **2.** As a class, brainstorm various nouns – people, places, animals and things. **3.** Write the dictated nouns in the blank noun box on the board. **4.** Students complete activities 1, 2 and the Common Words activity in their books.
Day 5	Assessment	Visual and phonological		**1.** Reinforce concepts and skills taught during the week. **2.** Dictate the ten spelling words to students. **3.** Record any relevant assessment information, for example, common errors made by students. **4.** After finishing the spelling test, students can complete the Rhyme time activity to extend comprehension skills.

Unit 1

FOCUS > Letter names and sounds – a b c d e f g h i j

1 Look at these words and pictures. Read the words. Say the beginning sound of each word.

2 Copy this table into your book.
Write words from above into the correct beginning sound box.

a	b	c	d	e	f	g	h	i	j
______	______	______	______	______	______	______	______	______	______

Off the page

- Choose two words beginning with the letter 'b'. Write them in a sentence in your book.
- Choose two words that begin with the same letter as your name. Write them in a sentence in your book.

3 Look at the pictures. Work out the beginning sound for each word.
Write the words in your book.

4 Copy this table into your book.
Write a word from above for the beginning sound in each box.

a pple	e ________	d ________	f ________	g ________
b ________	c ________	h ________	i ________	j ________

5 Choose two words from the table above and write them in sentences in your book.

WORD KNOWLEDGE > Alphabet

Upper case letters

1 Copy this table into your book.
Put the letters in alphabetical order in the table.
Which letters are missing? Write them in your book.

Q W E R T Y U I A S D F G H J K L Z X C B N V

Lower case letters

2 Copy this table into your book.
Put the letters in alphabetical order in the table.
Which letters are missing? Write them in your book.

p i y t r q a d g j k h f l z c e b m v x o w

Writing activity

- Write these animals in alphabetical order in your book.
  Write a sentence about one of these animals.

- Write the names of your family in alphabetical order in your book.

FOCUS > Letter names and sounds – k l m n o p q r

1 Look at these words and pictures. Read the words. Say the beginning sound of each word.

ladder 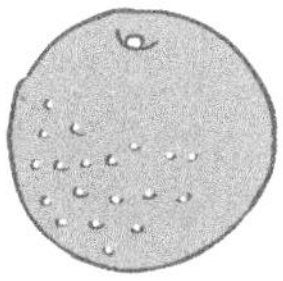 orange  king  octopus

key  nest  quack  rose 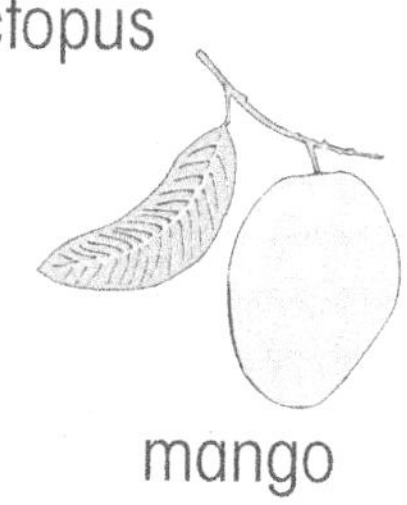 mango

queen 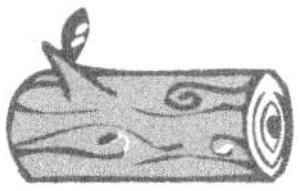 log  pumpkin  pan

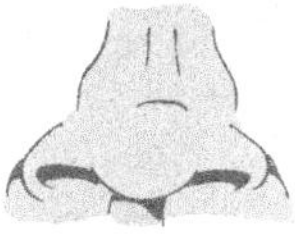

nose  leg  rabbit  moon

2 Copy this table into your book.
Write words from above into the correct beginning sound box.

k	l	m	n	o	p	q	r

Off the page

- Choose two words beginning with the letter 'm'. Write them in a sentence in your book.
- Choose two words that begin with the same letter as your mother's name. Write them in a sentence in your book.

3 Look at the pictures. Work out the beginning sound for each word.
Write the words in your book.

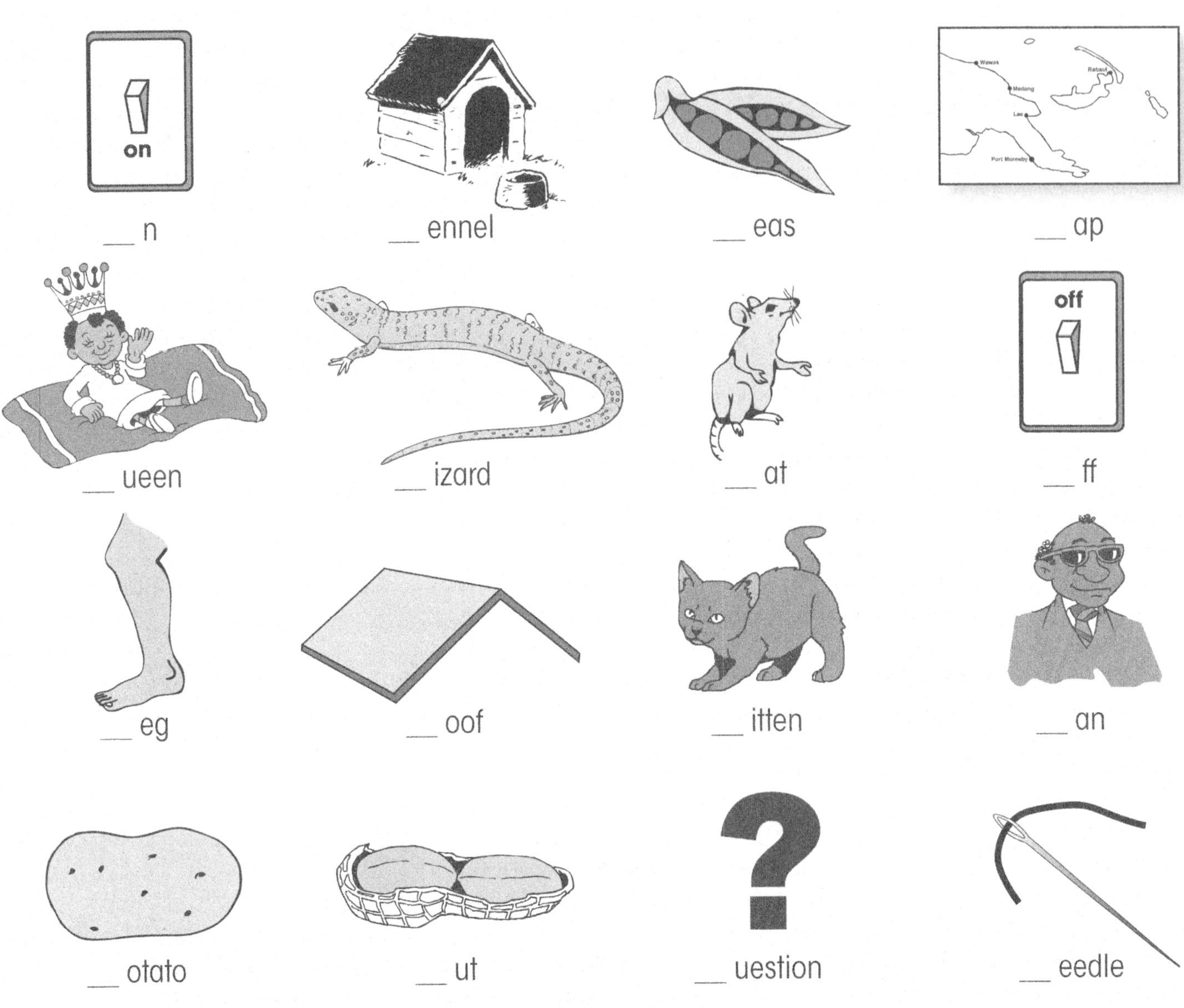

4 Copy this table into your book.
Write a word from above for the beginning sound in each box.

p *otato*	k ______	q ______	n ______
m ______	o ______	l ______	r ______

WORD KNOWLEDGE > Alphabet

A B C D E F G H I J K L M N O P Q R S T U V W X Y Z
a b c d e f g h i j k l m n o p q r s t u v w x y z

1 Copy this path into your book. Make sure you have drawn 26 steps.
Write the **lower case** letters of the alphabet in the steps. Begin with '**a**' and end with '**z**'.

2 Copy this track into your book. Write the **upper case** letters of the alphabet on the track.
Begin with A and end with Z.

3 Copy this table into your book. Write the letters below into the correct box.

w c O n E g h I x F S u z W P k d a T M u Q q L x o

lower case	UPPER CASE

Writing activity

- Draw a picture of yourself. Write your full name next to the picture.
(Don't forget to start with a capital letter.) Write a sentence or two about your picture.

This is me. I like swimming.
Angelo Somave

Unit 3

FOCUS > Letter names and sounds – s t u v w x y z

1 Look at these words and pictures. Read the words. Say the beginning sound of each word.

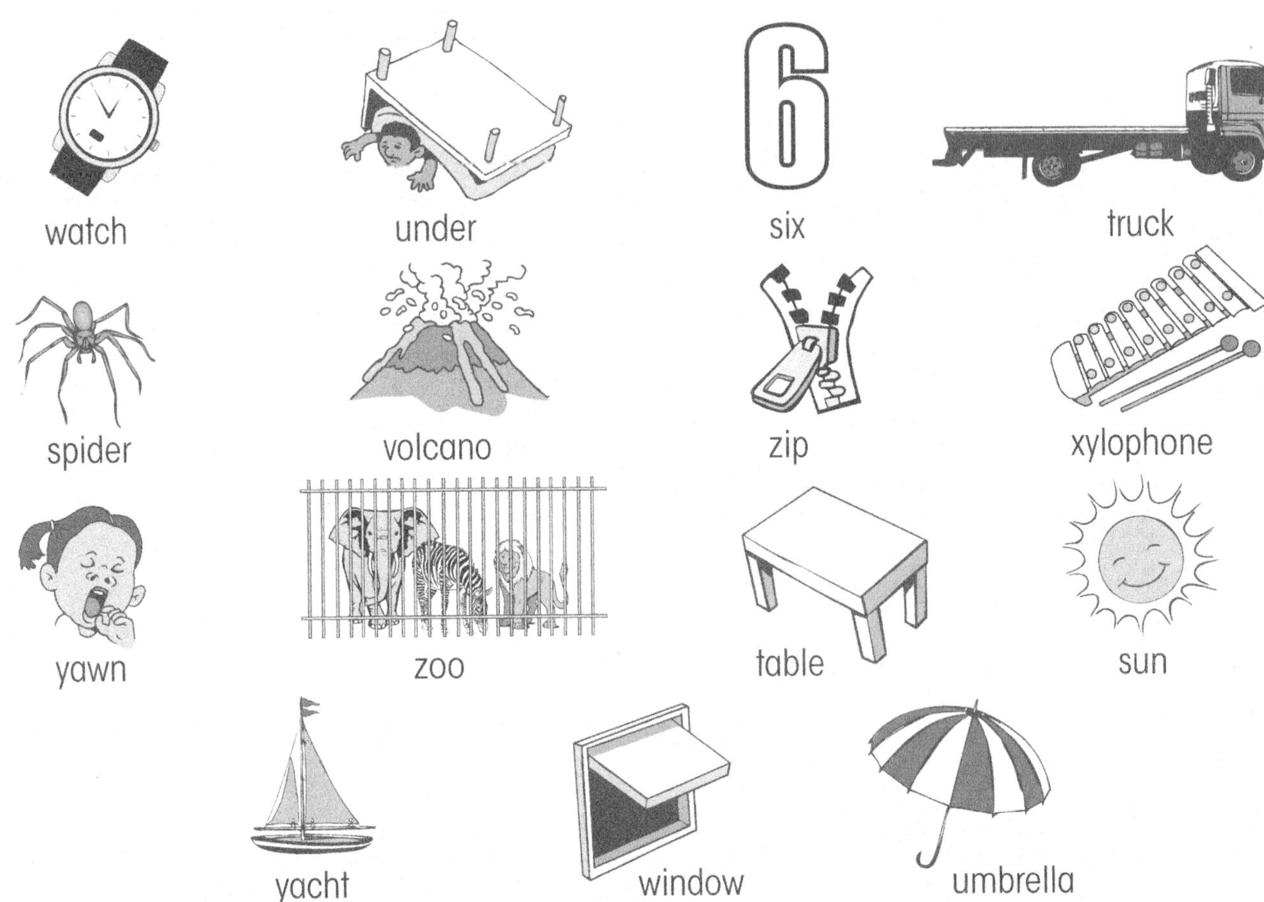

2 Copy this table into your book.
Write words from above into the correct beginning sound box.

s	t	u	v	w	x	y	z
______	______	______	______	______	______	______	______

Off the page

- Choose two words beginning with the letter 's'. Write them in a sentence in your book.
- Choose two words that begin with the same letter as your father's name. Write them in a sentence in your book.

3 Look at the pictures. Work out the beginning sound for each word. Write the words in your book.

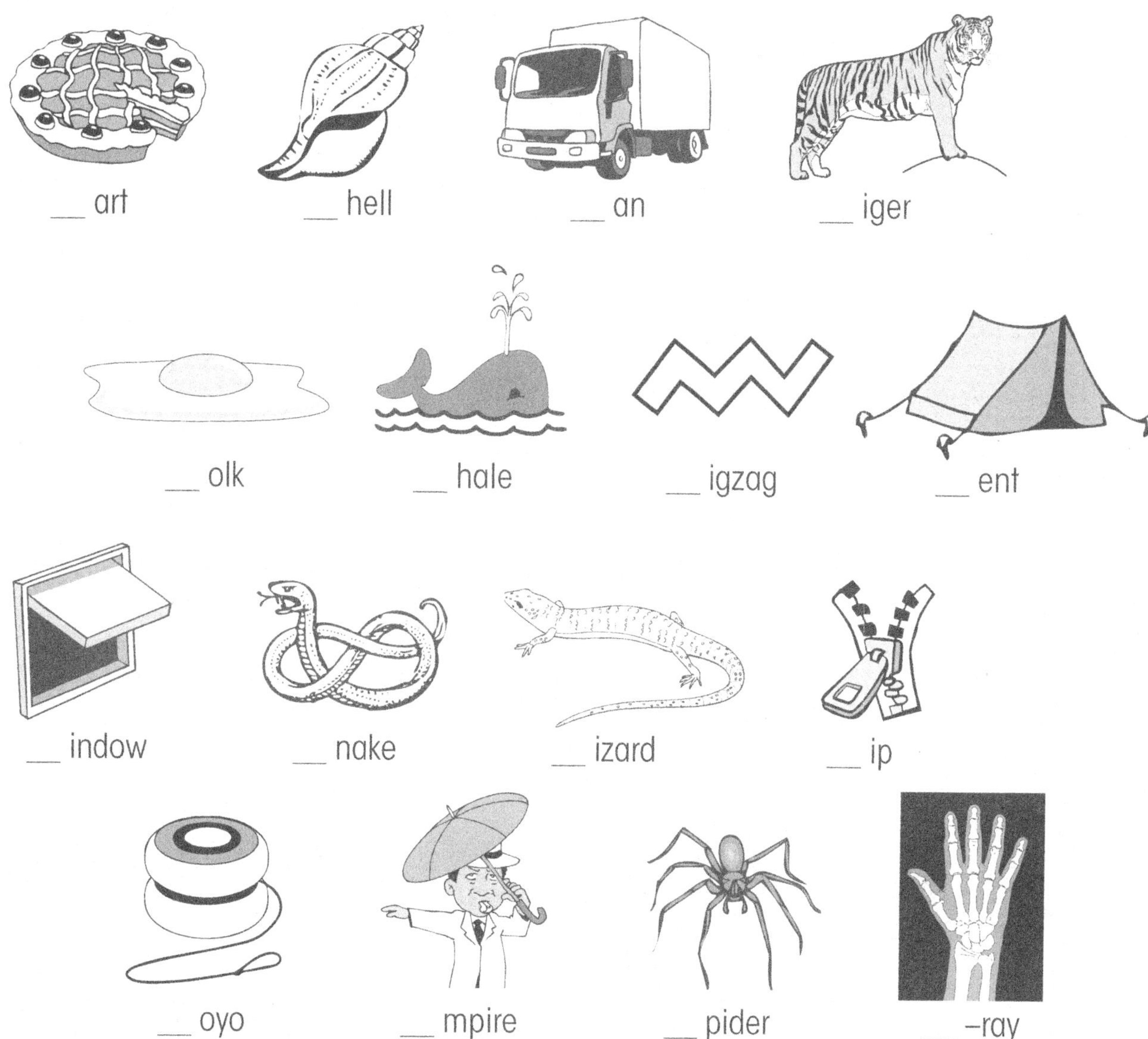

4 Copy this table into your book.
Write a word from above for the beginning sound in each box.

s *nake*	y ______	t ______	w ______
x ______	v ______	u ______	z ______

5 Choose two words from the table above and write them in sentences in your book.

WORD KNOWLEDGE > Alphabet

A B C D E F G H I J K L M N O P Q R S T U V W X Y Z
a b c d e f g h i j k l m n o p q r s t u v w x y z

Write the names of people, places or things that start with upper case letters in your book.

A friend ______________________ A teacher ______________________

A day of the week ______________________ A month of the year ______________________

A town ______________________ A province ______________________

A river ______________________ A country ______________________

Writing activity

- The zookeeper is trying to find the animal that does not belong in the zoo. Write the animals in alphabetical order in your book to help him.

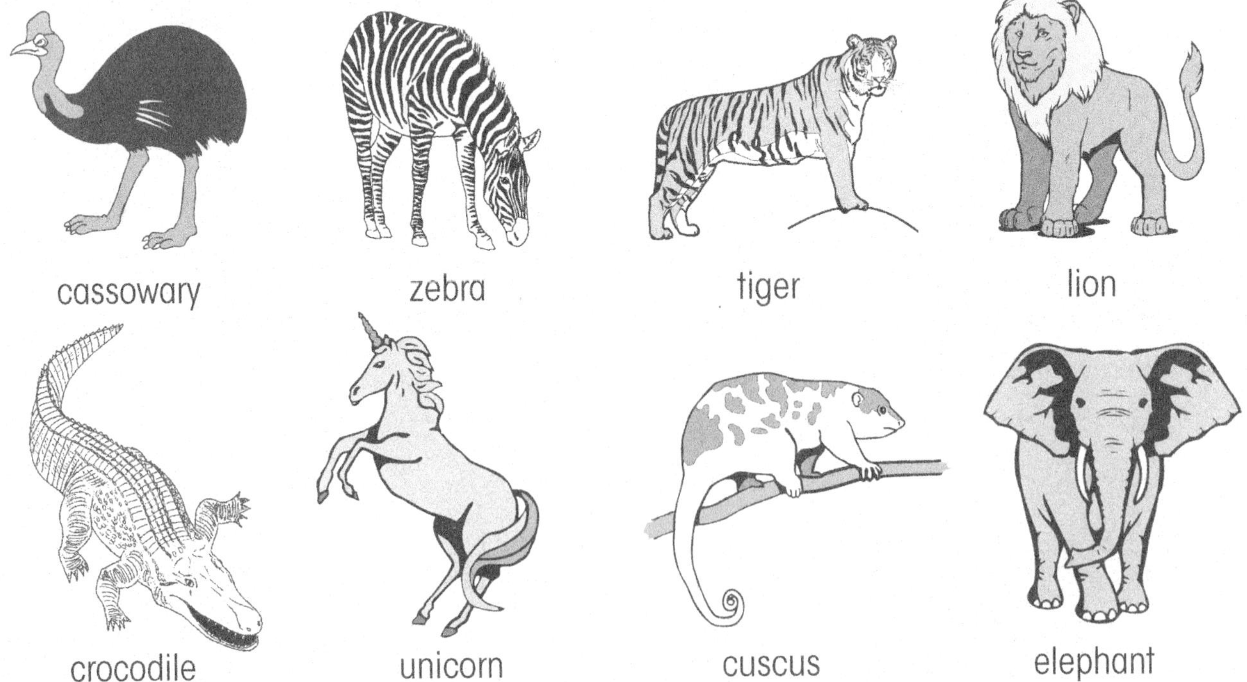

- Which animal does not belong to the zoo?
- Write four more animals that you would like to have in the zoo in alphabetical order in your book.

Unit 4

Revision

FOCUS > Revise letter names and sounds – a b c d e f g h i j k l m n o p q r s t u v w x y z

a	*arrow*
b	
c	
d	
e	
f	
g	

1 Copy this table into your book. Make spaces for all 26 letters. Look at the pictures and read the words below. Write the words into the correct row of the table. (The first one has been done for you.)

2 Did you have a word for every letter? Circle the letters that have more than one word. Underline the letters with no words. Can you write your own words for those letters?

FOCUS > Lower case letter order

1 Copy this letter snake into your book. Make sure it has 26 parts.
Write the 26 letters of the alphabet in lower case in the correct order on the snake.

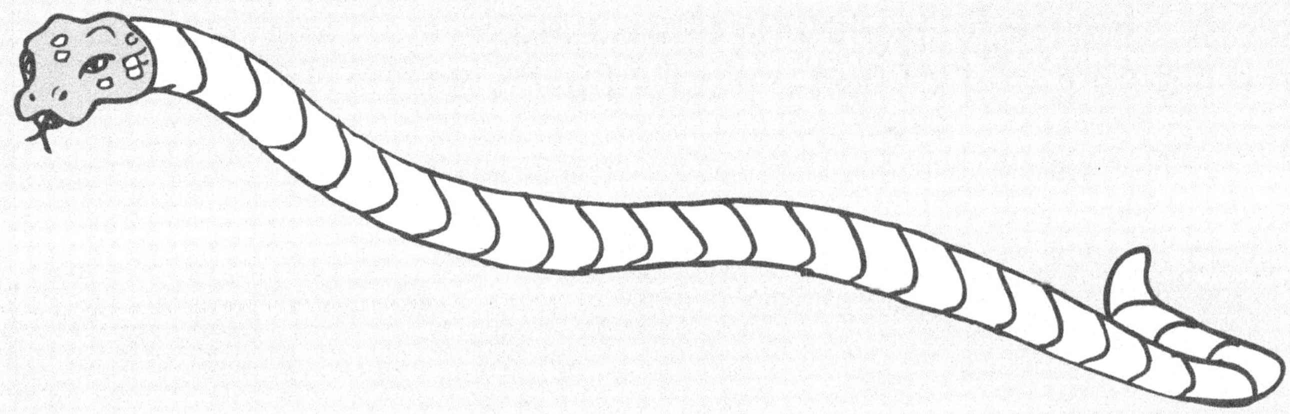

2 Draw a circle around these letters on your snake: f, t, j, s, b, h, r, u, p.

FOCUS > Upper case letter order

1 Copy this table into your book.
Write the words from the Word Bank into the correct box in alphabetical order.

UPPER CASE	Lower case

Word BANK

teacher Port Moresby Goroka jug girl
Mr Potek window hat July Tuesday

2 Look at the line of letters below. Copy it into your book.
Circle the lower case letters. Draw a square around the upper case letters.

a b C D e f G H i J K L m n o p Q R s T u V W x Y Z

Unit 5

FOCUS > Medial sound 'a'

Word LIST

ban
tan
can
fan
man
pan
ran
van
nan
bat
fat
sat
mat
rat
hat
cat
gap
sap
tap
cap
zap
lap
map

1 Find '**–an**' words from the Word List for these pictures.
Write the words in your book.

2 Find '**–at**' words from the Word List for these pictures.
Write the words in your book.

3 Find '**–ap**' words from the Word List for these pictures.
Write the words in your book.

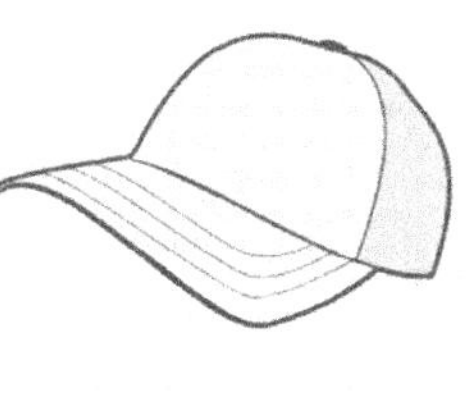
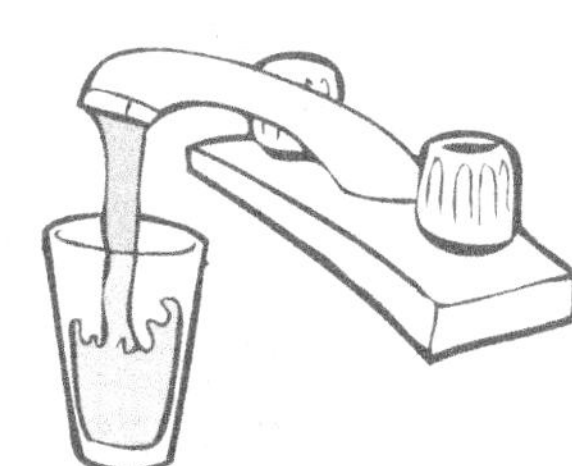
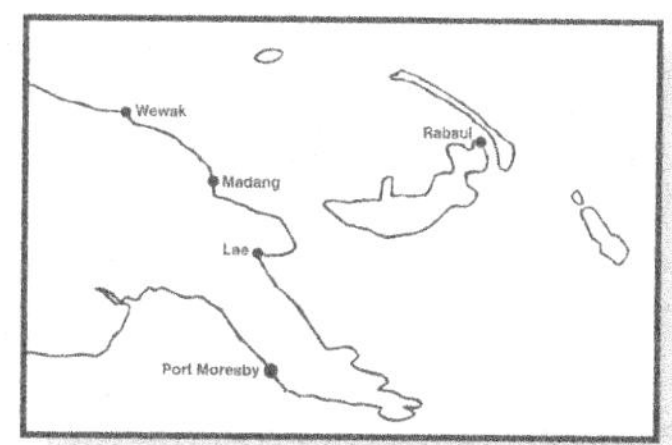

Off the page

- Write all the words that you know that rhyme with '**–an**' in your book.

4 Copy the hats into your book.
Write the words from the Word Bank into the correct hat.

HINT
The '–am' words go into the '–am' hat.

–am

–ad

Word BANK

dad dam jam rag wag ham sag pad lad bag yam sad

5 Write as many words as you can using the magic word machine, for example: y + am = yam.

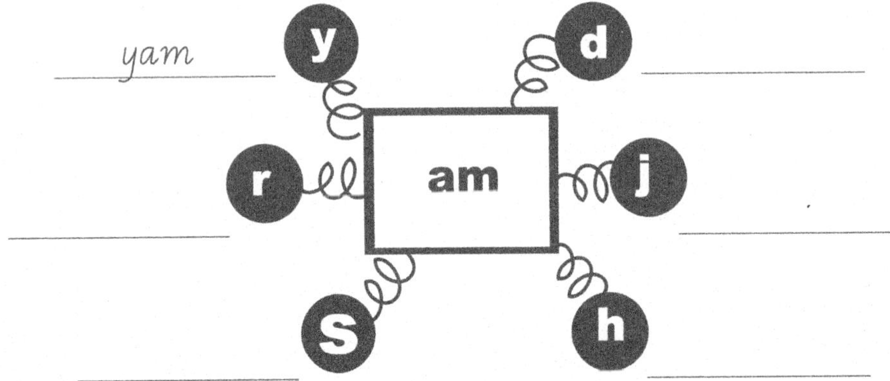

6 Copy this snake into your book.
Write all the '**–ap**' words that you can think of into the snake.

Word LIST

cap
gap
lap
map
rap
sap
tap
yap
zap
bad
dad
fad
had
lad
mad
pad
sad
dam
ham
jam
Pam
ram
Sam
yam

WORD KNOWLEDGE > Alphabet

1 Write these letters in alphabetical order in your book.

p i y t r q a d g j k h f l c e b m v o x n

2 Which letters are missing? Write them in your book.

3 Copy this table into your book.
Complete it with your own name and the names of two friends.

Letters in the names	Letters NOT in the names
Joseph	*a, b, c, d, f, g, i, k, l, m, n, q, r, t, u, v, w, x, y, z*

COMMON WORDS >

Choose words from the Spelling List to fill the gaps.
Write the complete sentences in your book.

1. My ____ is tall.
2. Can ____ see the van?
3. I like ____ red hat.
4. Sam ____ Dad went fishing.

Weekly Spelling List to be tested at the end of the week

Spelling LIST

pan
cat
bag
jam
dad
you
that
and
it
the

LOOK, COVER, WRITE, CHECK

Practise your weekly Spelling List this way:
1. LOOK carefully at the word.
2. COVER the word.
3. WRITE the word from memory.
4. CHECK to see if your spelling is correct.

Writing activity

- Write five interesting sentences in your book using words from the Spelling List.

Unit 6

FOCUS > Medial sound 'e'

Word LIST

red
bed
led
fed
sped
wed
sled
pen
hen
ten
men
den
met
pet
wet
net
vet
set

1 Find '**–ed**' words from the Word List for these pictures.
Write the words in your book.

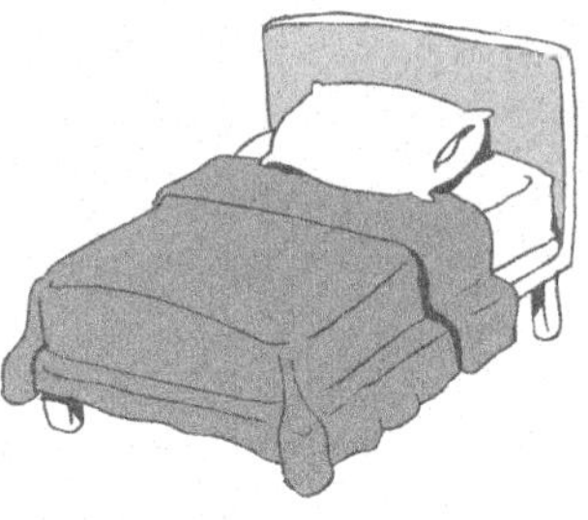

2 Find '**–en**' words from the Word List for these pictures.
Write the words in your book.

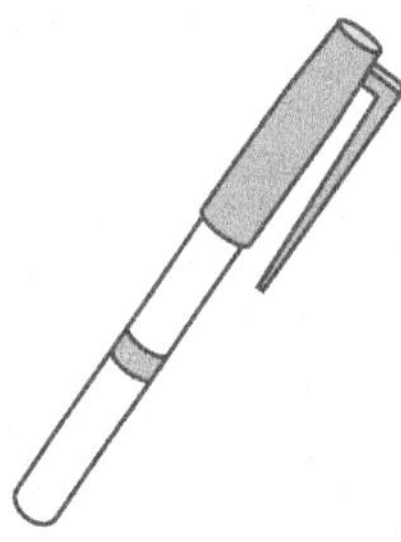

10

3 Find '**–et**' words from the Word List for these pictures.
Write the words in your book.

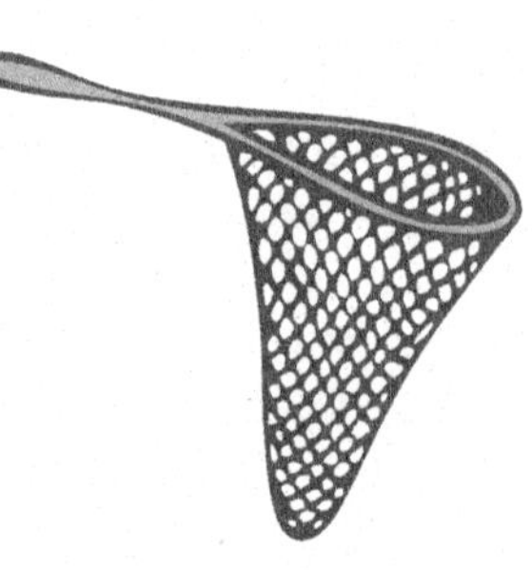

Off the page

- Write all the words that you know that rhyme with '**–ell**' in your book.

4 Copy the nets.
Write the words from the Word Bank into the correct net.

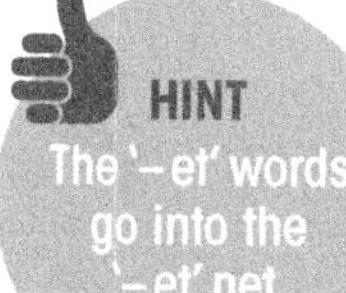

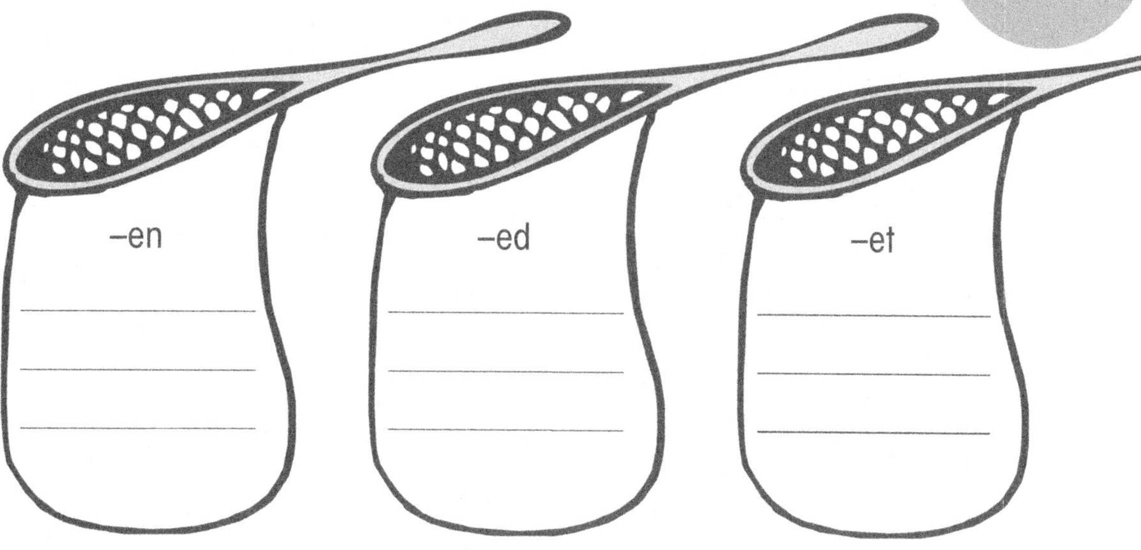

Word BANK

hen red net wed fed pet ten bet led wet men pen

Word LIST

bed
fed
led
red
wed
sled
sped
bet
get
jet
let
met
net
pet
set
vet
wet
yet
den
fen
hen
men
pen
ten
yen
beg
egg
keg
leg
peg

5 Use the word wheel to make words with '**e**' in the middle.
Write the words in your book.

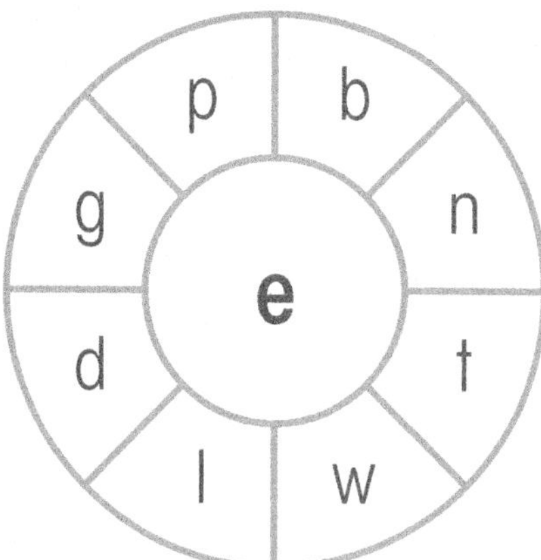

6 Copy this table into your book.
Write the '**e**' words from the word wheel into the correct box.

–et	–eg	–ed	–eb	–en

WORD KNOWLEDGE > Alphabet

1 Write these letters in alphabetical order in your book.

v o x n h f l c r q a d g j k p i y t e b m

2 Which letters are missing? Write them in your book.

3 Copy this table into your book.
Complete it with the names of three people in your family.

Letters in the names	Letters NOT in the names
Margaret	b, c, d, f, h, i, j, k, l, n, o, p, q, s, u, v, w, x, y, z

COMMON WORDS >

1 Choose words from the Spelling List to fill the gaps.
Write the complete sentences in your book.

a. The ___ ___ ___ laid an egg.

b. Ring the ___ ___ ___ ___ to come inside.

c. I have ___ ___ ___ ___ fingers and one thumb.

d. We ___ ___ ___ going to the zoo.

e. The ___ ___ ___ ___ is in the net.

2 Copy these words into your book.
Write a sentence for each word.

are fish four me

Weekly Spelling List to be tested at the end of the week

Spelling LIST

bed
hen
net
leg
bell
me
are
we
four
fish

Writing activity

■ Draw four hens in your book. Write an '**–en**' word in each hen.

Unit 7

FOCUS > Medial sound 'i'

Word LIST

dip
zip
pip
drip
slip
ship
trip
sip
rip
win
bin
fin
skin
grin
pin
did
lid
rid
slid
kid
hid

1 Find '**–ip**' words from the Word List for these pictures.
Write the words in your book.

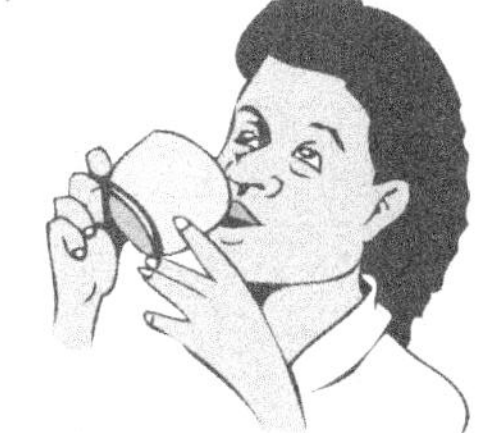

2 Find '**–in**' words from the Word List for these pictures.
Write the words in your book.

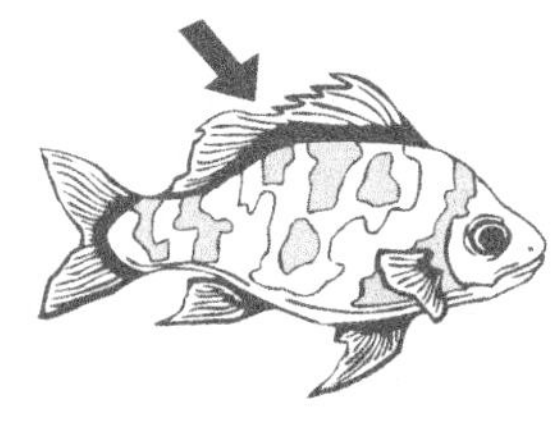

3 Find '**–id**' words from the Word List for these pictures.
Write the words in your book.

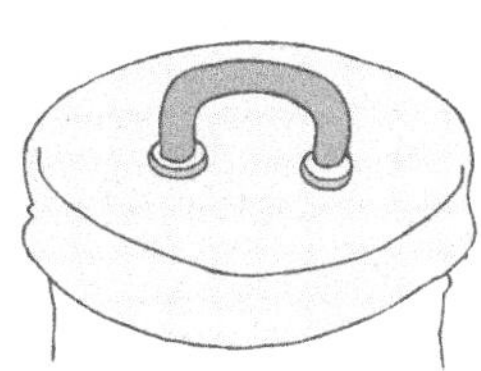

Off the page

- Write all the words that you know that rhyme with '**–ig**' in your book.

4 Copy the tins into your book.
Write the words from the Word Bank into the correct tin.

HINT The '–in' words go into the '–in' tin.

Word BANK

lid big pig in rid skin tin kid win did jig rig

5 Copy this pig into your book. Write all the '**–ig**' words in the pig.

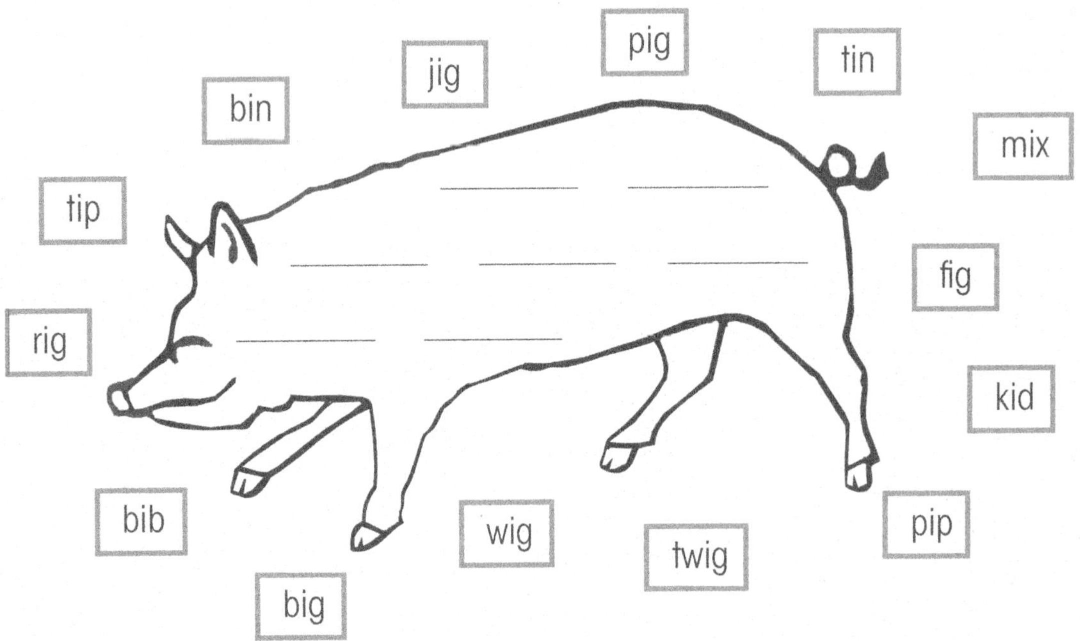

6 Write each of these words in a sentence in your book.

pip slid bin six

Word LIST

bid	big
did	dig
hid	fig
kid	gig
lid	jig
rid	pig
skid	rig
slid	wig
dip	twig
hip	bin
lip	fin
pip	grin
rip	kin
sip	pin
tip	skin
trip	tin
zip	win
bib	fix
fib	mix
jib	six
rib	
crib	
bit	
fit	
hit	
kit	
lit	
pit	
sit	
wit	

WORD KNOWLEDGE > Vowels – a e i o u

1 Copy this table into your book.
Write the words from the Vowel Box into the correct box.

a	e	i	o	u
apple	elephant	igloo	octopus	umbrella

Vowel BOX

ant egg ostrich under axe eskimo orange unhappy insect imp

2 Copy this path into your book. Write the letters of the alphabet in the path.
Make the vowels red and the other letters blue.

Weekly Spelling List to be tested at the end of the week

COMMON WORDS >

Choose words from the Spelling List to fill the gaps.
Write the complete sentences in your book.

1. You are big, __ __ __ Letti is bigger.
2. We __ __ __ __ to go now.
3. The black horse will __ __ __ the race.
4. I want you to come __ __ __ __ me.
5. They will __ __ late for school.

Spelling LIST

dip
win
slid
pin
ship
but
with
be
have
am

Writing activity

■ Write each of these words in a sentence in your book: dip ship have am

Unit 8

FOCUS > Medial sound 'o'

Word LIST

not
pot
dot
trot
hot
got
cot
tot
hop
top
chop
stop
mop
pop
bog
fog
log
dog
jog
frog

1 Find '**–ot**' words from the Word List for these pictures. Write the words in your book.

2 Find '**–op**' words from the Word List for these pictures. Write the words in your book.

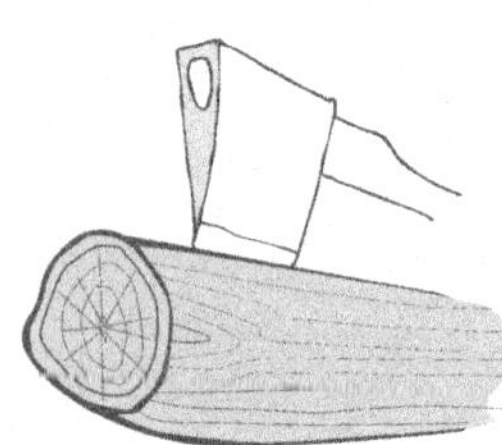

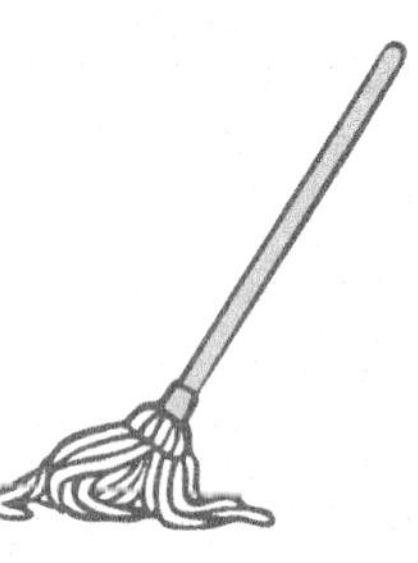

3 Find '**–og**' words from the Word List for these pictures. Write the words in your book.

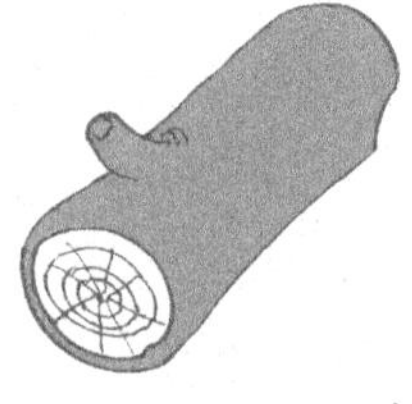

Off the page

- Write all the words that you know that rhyme with '**–ob**' in your book.

4 Copy the pots in your book.
Write the words from the Word Bank into the correct pot.

HINT
The '–ot' words go into the '–ot' pot.

Word BANK

top not mob sob rot pop hop cot job mop hot rob

5 Make as many three-letter words as you can with the magic word machine, for example: c + o + t = cot.

MAGIC WORD MACHINE

Beginning sounds	Middle sounds	End sounds
c r h s m p t d b c j l n	o	p b t d g

6 Copy this table into your book.
Sort the words from the Word List into the box.
Can you write words that are not in the Word List?

–op	–ob	–ot	–od	–og

Word LIST

cop
hop
lop
mop
pop
top
stop
chop
crop
bob
cob
job
lob
mob
rob
sob
cot
dot
hot
got
jot
lot
not
rot
tot
slot
trot
cod
god
nod
pod
rod
plod

WORD KNOWLEDGE › Vowels – a e i o u

1 Write these words in your book.
Underline the vowel at the beginning of each word.
The first one has been done for you.

a	e	i	o	u
apple	elephant	ice cream	octopus	umbrella
ant	egg	ink	orange	umpire
arrow	end	igloo	off	under

2 Copy these boxes into your book.
Write five vowels in the small box. Write 21 consonants in the big box.
How many letters are in both boxes?

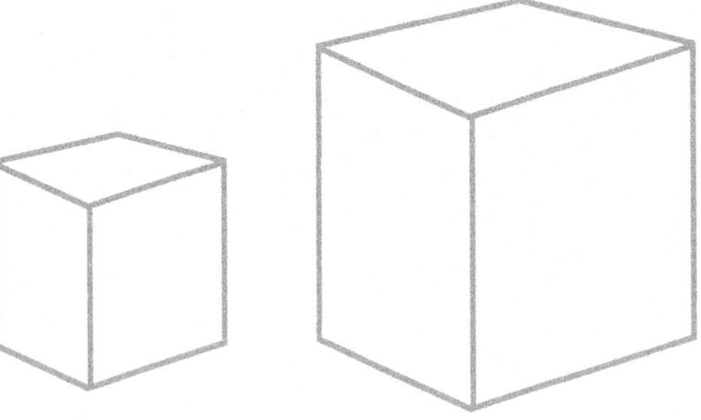

COMMON WORDS ›

Choose words from the Spelling List to fill the gaps.
Write the complete sentences in your book.

1. The red light means _ _ _ _ .
2. Jack and Jill went _ _ the hill.
3. He stepped _ _ to the bus.
4. Lai likes to go into the lolly _ _ _ _ .
5. The _ _ _ sat on the mat.

Spelling LIS

rob
pot
dog
stop
box
shop
had
up
on
can

Writing activity

- Write five things that can be turned 'on' or 'off', such as a light.
  Write a sentence that includes both words.

FOCUS > Medial sound 'u'

1 Find '**–ug**' words from the Word List for these pictures.
Write the words in your book.

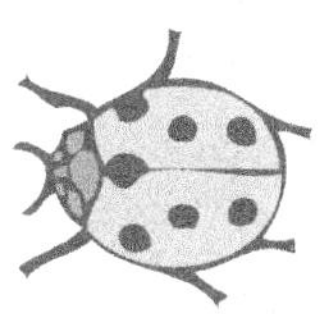

2 Find '**–un**' words from the Word List for these pictures.
Write the words in your book.

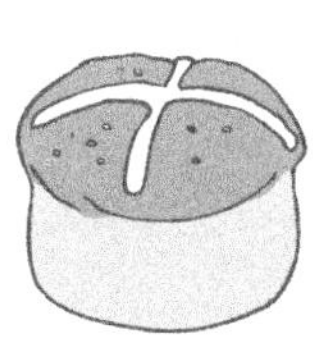

3 Find '**–um**' words from the Word List for these pictures.
Write the words in your book.

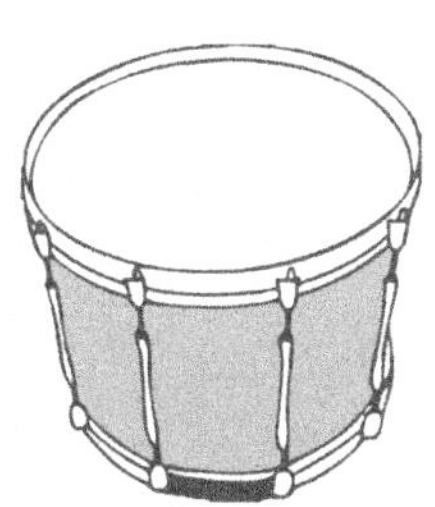
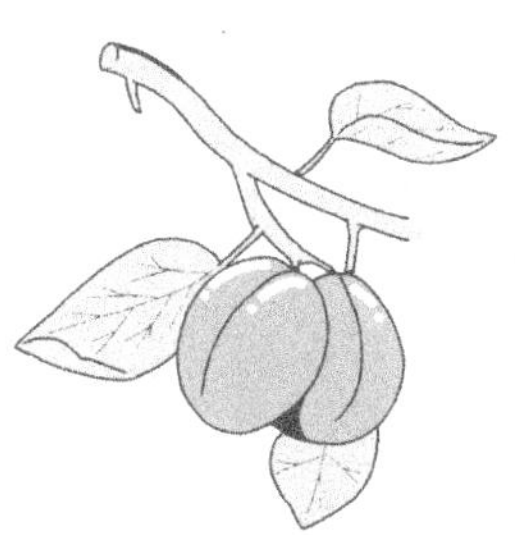
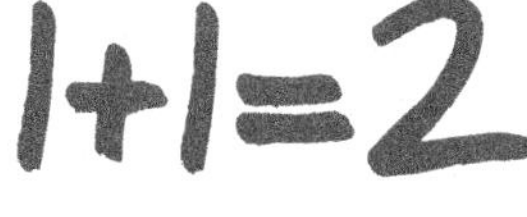

Word LIST

mug
dug
jug
tug
bug
plug
hug
rug
fun
spun
sun
bun
run
hum
plum
sum
gum
drum
mum

Off the page

- Write all the words that you know that rhyme with '**–ut**' in your book.

4 Copy the mugs into your book.
Write the words from the Word Bank into the correct mug.

HINT
The '–ug' words go into the '–ug' jug.

Word BANK

sun gum rug tug plum run plug swum bun fun

5 Copy this table into your book.
Use letters from the word wheel to make words with 'u' in the middle.

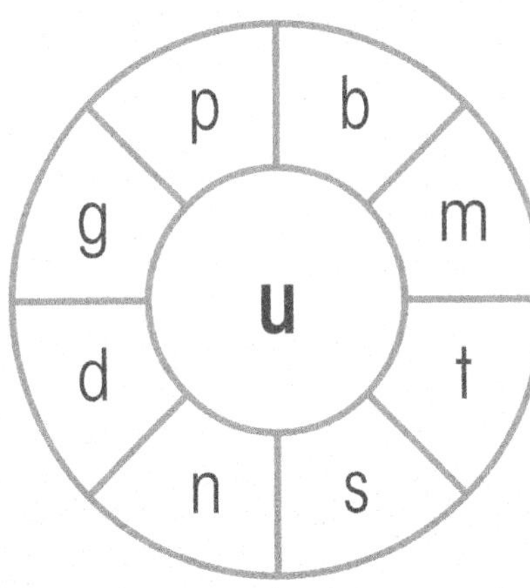

6 Copy this table into your book.
Write the 'u' words from the word wheel into the correct box.

–ug	–ud	–un	–um

Word LIST

bug	bun
dug	fun
hug	gun
jug	nun
mug	run
rug	sun
tug	shu
drug	spu
glug	stu
plug	but
slug	cut
smug	hut
snug	nut
thug	cu
gum	pu
hum	up
rum	bu
sum	du
glum	mu
plum	
scum	
slum	
swum	

WORD KNOWLEDGE › Compound words

RULE

Compound words are made when two smaller words are joined to make a bigger word.
For example: *sun + set = sunset, sun + light = sunlight.*

1 Write compound words beginning with the word 'sun' in your book.

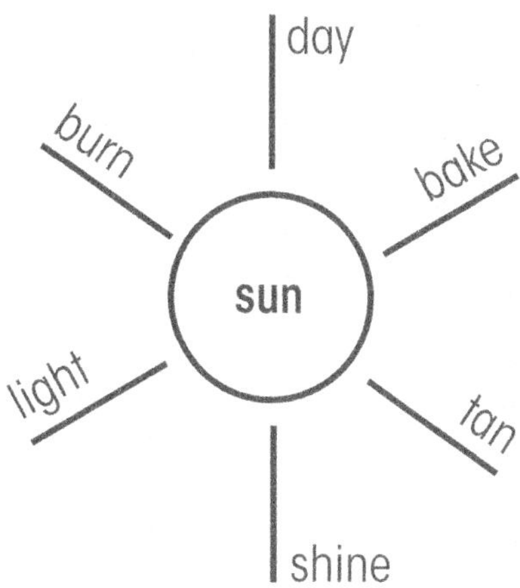

2 Write compound words beginning with the word 'play' in your book.
Use the words in the Word Bank to help you, for example: play + time = playtime.

Word BANK

time school room ground mate

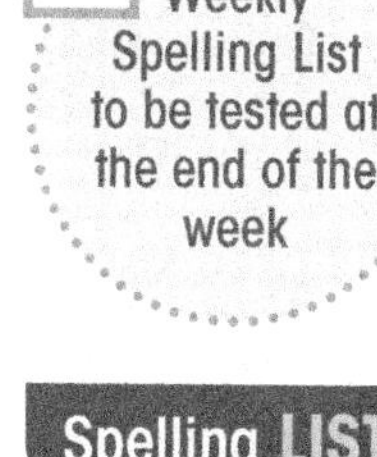

COMMON WORDS ›

Choose words from the Spelling List to fill the gaps.
Write the complete sentences in your book.

1. The _ _ _ of two plus two is four.
2. I think _ _ _ is the girl who won the race.
3. Can you tell me _ _ _ _ you will be here?
4. Look _ _ that big cat.
5. The little _ _ _ flew into the _ _ _ .

Spelling LIST

bug
jug
sun
nut
sum
is
she
they
when
at

Writing activity

■ Draw four slugs in your book. Write an '**–ug**' word in each slug.

Revision

FOCUS > Medial sounds 'a' 'e' 'i' 'o' 'u'

1 Copy this table into your book.
Write the words from the Word Bank into the correct box.

'a' sound	'e' sound	'i' sound	'o' sound	'u' sound

Word BANK

pan jug leg jab sun pit bat man
mop bug hut pen pot did net rat

2 Use words from the Word Bank to fill the gaps. Write the complete sentences in your book.

a. Mum put the plant in the _ _ _.
b. Pour the milk from the _ _ _.
c. The _ _ _ put on his trousers.
d. She broke her _ _ _ .
e. The _ _ _ has a sharp point.

3 Write these words in a sentence in your book.

dog big rat

4 Copy this table into your book. Make up your own words to complete the table.

'–at' words	'–et' words	'–ig' words	'–op' words	'–un' words
rat	*jet*	*pig*	*pop*	*bun*
sat	*pet*	*jig*	*hop*	*spun*

5 Copy these tables into your book.
Use the word wheels to write 'a', 'e', 'i', 'o' and 'u' words in the tables.

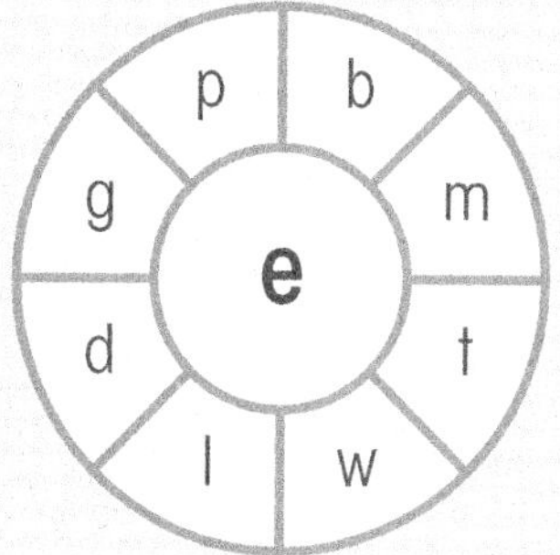

–ag	–at	–an
r a g	b a t	t a n
___ ___ ___	___ ___ ___	___ ___ ___
___ ___ ___	___ ___ ___	___ ___ ___
___ ___ ___	___ ___ ___	___ ___ ___

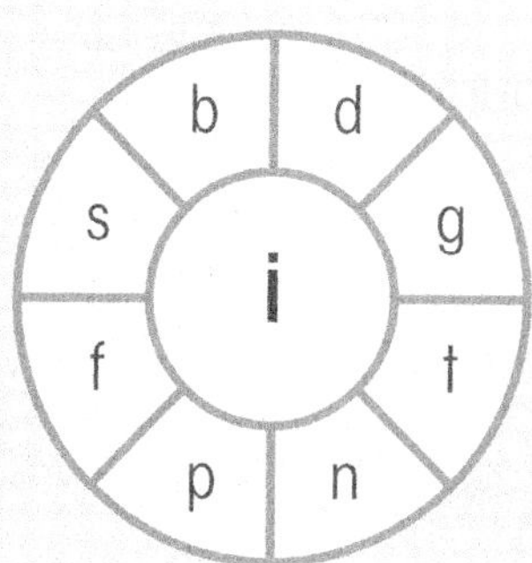

–et	–ed	–eg
w e t	w e d	___ ___ ___
___ ___ ___	___ ___ ___	___ ___ ___
___ ___ ___	___ ___ ___	___ ___ ___
___ ___ ___	___ ___ ___	___ ___ ___

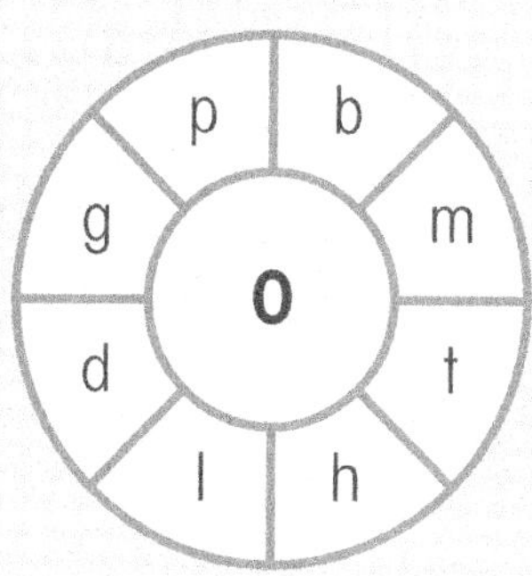

–ig	–in	–ip
f i g	p i n	p i p
___ ___ ___	___ ___ ___	___ ___ ___
___ ___ ___	___ ___ ___	___ ___ ___
___ ___ ___	___ ___ ___	___ ___ ___

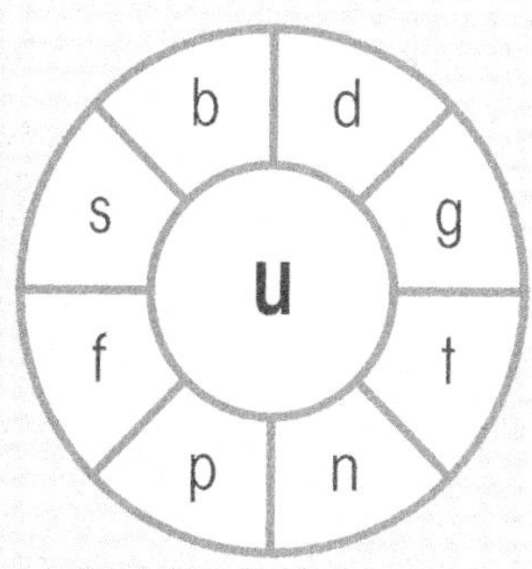

–op	–ot	–ob
___ ___ ___	l o t	m o b
___ ___ ___	___ ___ ___	___ ___ ___
___ ___ ___	___ ___ ___	___ ___ ___
___ ___ ___	___ ___ ___	___ ___ ___

u
b d s g f t p n

–un	–ut	–ug
b u n	___ ___ ___	t u g
___ ___ ___	___ ___ ___	___ ___ ___
___ ___ ___	___ ___ ___	___ ___ ___
___ ___ ___	___ ___ ___	___ ___ ___

Unit 11

FOCUS > '–nd' words

1 Copy this table into your book.
Write the words from the Word Bank into the correct box.

–and	–end	–ond

Word BANK

pan hand mend bend land bond band
send lend pond stand blend blond

2 Find the words for these pictures in the Word List. Write the words in your book.

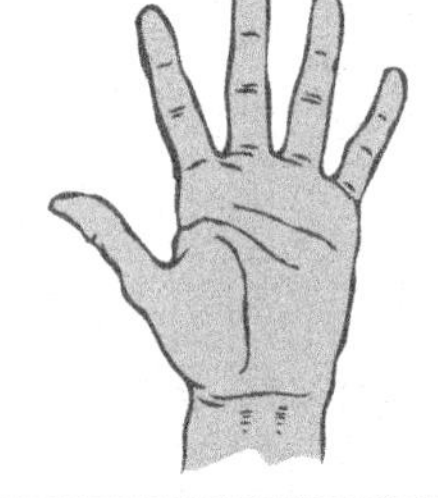

3 Use the '**–end**' and '**–and**' stars to write '**–end**' and '**–and**' words in your book.

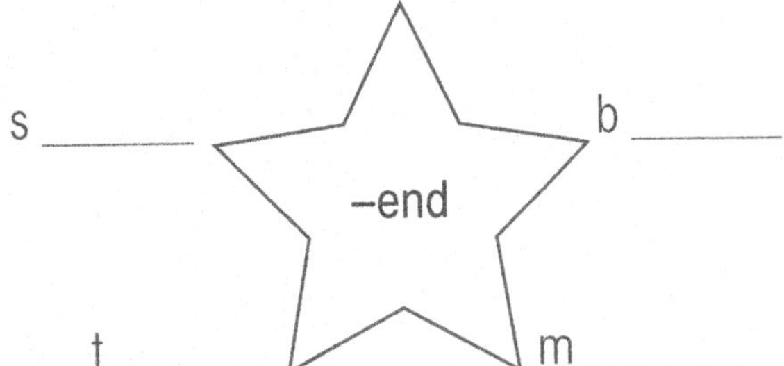

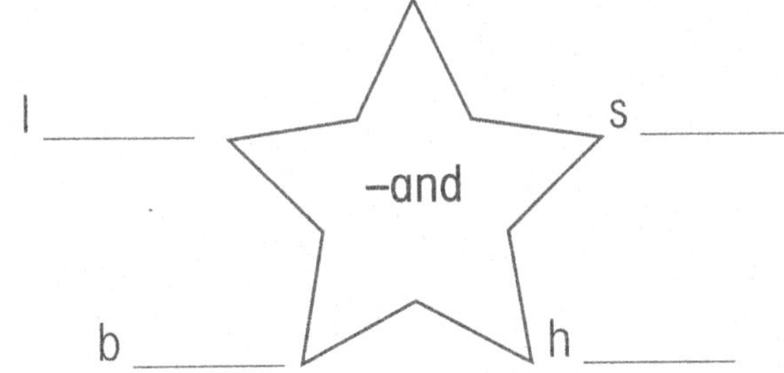

Word LIST

band
hand
land
sand
bland
brand
gland
grand
stand
bend
fend
lend
mend
send
tend
blend
wind
bond
fond
pond
blond
frond

Off the page

■ Trace your hand in your book. Write an '**–and**' word on each finger of your hand.

4 Use words from the Word List to fill the gaps.
Write the complete sentences in your book.

a. My _ _ _ _ has five fingers.

b. Ducks swim in a _ _ _ _ .

c. The _ _ _ _ blew the leaves away.

d. Flo has black hair and Che has _ _ _ _ _ hair.

e. I will _ _ _ _ her an email.

f. The _ _ _ _ played a marching song.

g. We came to a _ _ _ _ in the river.

5 Choose the correct word. Write the complete sentences in your book.

a. The (sand / band) is in my shoes.

b. Can you (bend / mend) my torn shirt?

c. I saw three goldfish in the (pond / fond).

d. Mike can (sand / stand) on one leg.

e. Pick your spoon up with your right (hand / stand).

Word LIST

band
hand
land
sand
bland
brand
gland
grand
stand
bend
fend
lend
mend
send
tend
blend
wind
bond
fond
pond
blond
frond

RHYME time › Copy this rhyme into your book and then ...

Hand over hand,
Towards the sand,
We swam and swam and swam.
Hand in hand,
Over the sand,
We ran and ran and ran.

1. Circle all the words ending in '**–and**'.
2. Write sentences in your book with these words: grand, hand.
3. Write sentences in your book with these words: end, send.
4. Write a sentence in your book with this word: wind.

WORD KNOWLEDGE > Nouns

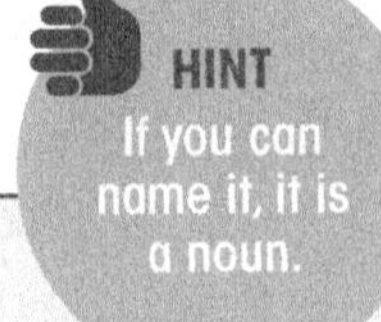

RULE

Nouns are the names of people, places, animals or things.
For example, *sand, pond* and *hand* are naming words.
All the words in the picture below are nouns. They are the names of things.

1 Write the names of some of the things you can see in this picture in your book.

2 Write these nouns in sentences in your book.

baby girl boy sand roof

COMMON WORDS >

Choose words from the Spelling List to fill the gaps.
Write the complete sentence in your book.

1. We are going _ _ _ for dinner.
2. The tadpole swam in the _ _ _ _ .
3. We _ _ _ _ on the bus.
4. I _ _ _ _ ice cream.
5. You can _ _ _ go to the zoo.

Spelling LIST

- I
- all
- like
- out
- were
- sand
- bend
- pond
- hand
- send

Writing activity

- Write five interesting sentences in your book, using words from the Spelling List.

FOCUS > '–ck' words

1 Draw this truck in your book. Write the '**–ck**' words in the truck.

2 Find the words for the pictures in the Word List. Write the words in your book.

Off the page

■ Write '**–ick**', '**–ack**', '**–ock**' and '**–uck**' words in sentences of your own.

Word LIST

quack
sack
tack
black
crack
back
Jack
tick
lick
sick
brick
stick
quick
chick
lock
clock
sock
frock
tock
rock
peck
wreck
deck
speck
neck
cluck
suck
tuck
stuck
truck
luck

3 Use the '–ick' and '–ock' clocks to write '–ick' and '–ock' words in your book.

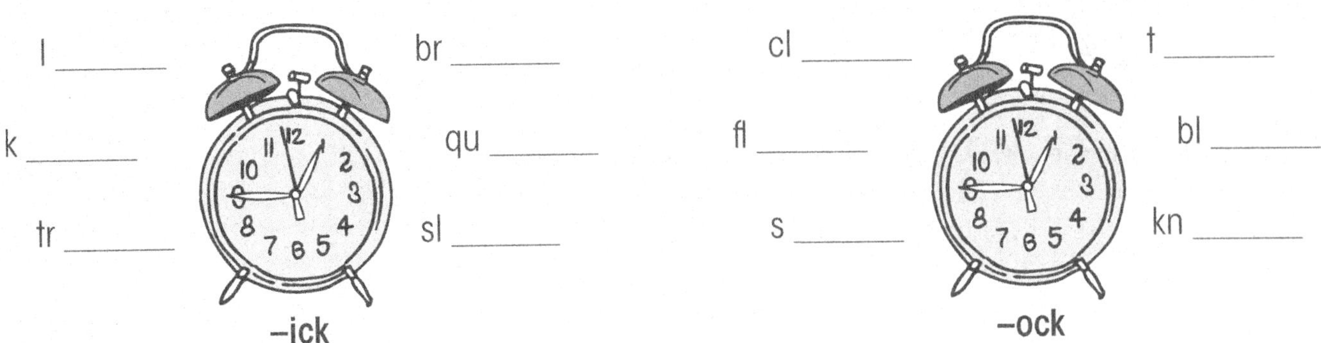

4 Copy this table into your book.
Write words from the Word Bank in the correct box.

–ack	–eck	–ick	–ock	–uck
______	______	______	______	______

5 Use words from the Word Bank to fill the gaps.
Write the complete sentences in your book.

a. The _ _ _ _ said, "Quack, quack quack."
b. You must not _ _ _ _ your thumb.
c. I heard the clock go _ _ _ _ tock.
d. Can you _ _ _ _ _ the stamp on the envelope?
e. I saw the rooster _ _ _ _ the chook.
f. Mum will _ _ _ _ my clothes for the holiday.
g. The _ _ _ _ of potatoes broke open.

6 Choose the correct word.
Write the complete sentences in your book.

a. The car was (stuck / sick) in the mud.
b. I saw the (pack / peck) of cards on the table.
c. My (deck / neck) is sore.
d. The (click / clock) struck one.
e. The (black / sock) had a hole in it.

Word BANK

duck
pick
sick
pack
sock
pluck
peck
clock
neck
jack
tick
stack
suck
sack
struck
stick

WORD KNOWLEDGE > Nouns

RULE

Remember that **nouns** are the names of people, places, animals and things.

1 Copy this table into your book.
Write the words from the Noun Box into the correct box.

People	Places	Animals	Things
			clock

2 Write these words in sentences in your book.

toys ball box clown doll

Noun BOX

Jack
rock
sock
Papua New Guinea
duck
Australia
clock
truck
neck
Jock
Lae
frock
chick
stick
Mick

COMMON WORDS >

Choose words from the Spelling List to fill the gaps.
Write complete sentences in your book.

1. You must not __ __ late for dinner.
2. Can you __ __ __ in the dark?
3. I like to __ __ __ fruit.
4. It was __ __ __ __ about time to go.
5. You are __ __ __ there yet.

Weekly Spelling List to be tested at the end of the week

Spelling LIST

be
just
not
see
eat
pack
neck
sick
lock
truck

RHYME time > Copy this rhyme into your book and then ...

Quick! Quick!
The cat's been sick,
And so has the dog,
And Jock, Jack and Nick!
This is bad luck
That so many are sick!
Poor cat, poor dog,
Poor Jock, Jack and Nick.

1. Underline the words ending in '**–ick**' in blue.
2. Underline the words ending in '**–ack**' in red.
3. Circle all the words ending in '**–ock**'.
4. Draw a square around the word ending in '**–uck**'.

FOCUS › '–nk' words

1 Copy the tank into your book. Write the '**–nk**' words in the tank.

sank | plum | pink | stop | drink | sink | swam | wink | box | tank

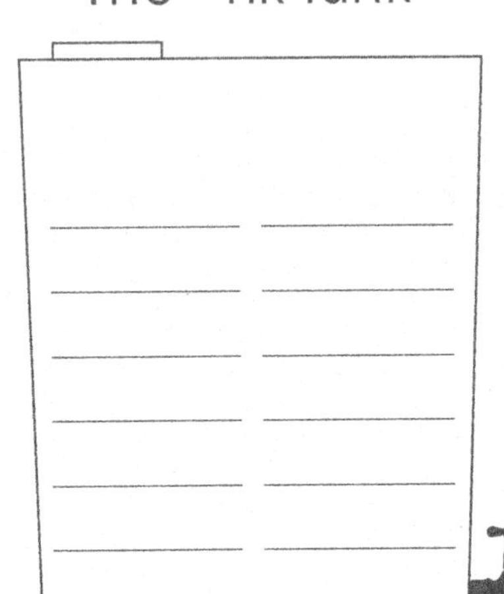

trip | bunk | trot | sunk | junk | drank | back | trunk | truck | stunk

2 Find the words for the pictures in the Word List. Write the words in your book.

3 Copy this plank into your book. Write '**–ank**' words in the plank.

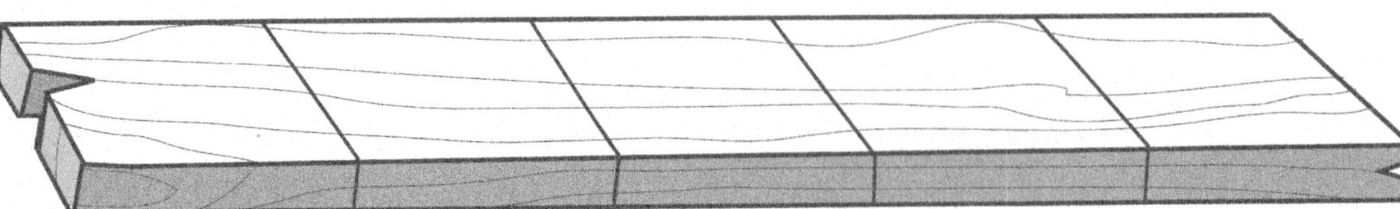

Word LIST

bank
sank
tank
yank
blank
crank
drank
plank
prank
shrank
spank
thank
pink
sink
wink
blink
clink
drink
shrink
slink
stink
think
kink
link
mink
rink

bunk
dunk
hunk
junk
sunk
chur
shru
skun
slun
spur
stun
trunk
flunk
plun

Off the page

■ Write a sentence in your book about what might happen to a pink drink on the sink.

4 Copy this table into your book.
Write the words from the Word Bank in the correct box.

–ank	–ink	–unk

Word BANK

thank bank shrink clink hunk pink sank chunk
link spank bunk wink junk blink drank

5 What is this boy doing?
Write a sentence about the picture in your book.
Use some '**–ink**' words in your sentence.

6 Find words from the Word Bank to fill the gaps.
Write the complete sentences in your book.

a. The ship _ _ _ _ in the bay.

b. There is a lot of _ _ _ _ in my room.

c. I _ _ _ _ _ two glasses of water.

d. The flowers are _ _ _ _ .

e. We went to the _ _ _ _ for some money.

7 Choose the correct word. Write the complete sentences in your book.

a. I want to (thank / think) you for the gift.

b. I went to sleep on the (bunk / chunk).

c. The dress will (clink / shrink) in water.

d. You must not (wink / spank) the little boy.

WORD KNOWLEDGE > Pronouns

RULE

Pronouns are used to take the place of nouns.

Pronoun Box

I
me
he
she
we
him
they
them
it
her

1 Choose words from the Pronoun Box to fill the gaps.
Write the complete sentences in your book.

a. John gave the book to m __.

b. We saw th __ __ on Sunday.

c. Please take h __ __ home.

d. She likes h __ __ new shoes.

2 Choose the correct word. Write the complete sentences in your book.

a. (We / it) are going to the play.

b. (He / they) is a tall boy.

c. What did you say to (he / them)?

d. I think (him / she) is at home.

COMMON WORDS >

Choose words from the Spelling List to fill the gaps.
Write the complete sentences in your book.

1. I don't know who __ __ __ it.
2. Shae's work is __ __ __ __ good.
3. She put on her coat and __ __ __ __ she went out.
4. Billy slept in, __ __ he was late.

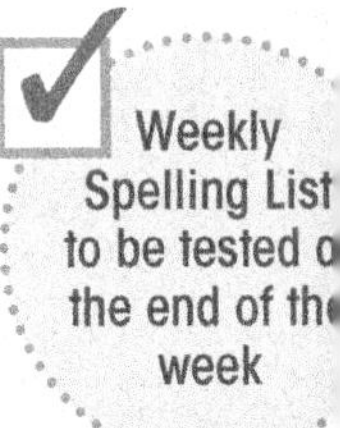

Weekly Spelling List to be tested o[n] the end of th[e] week

Spelling LIS[T]

if
so
then
very
did
tank
sink
trunk
thank
wink

RHYME time > Copy this rhyme into your book and then ...

Roses are red,
Violets are pink.
I wash my feet
In the kitchen sink.
The water's black,
My feet are pink,
I dip in my mug
And have a long drink.

1. Circle all the words that rhyme with 'pink'.
2. Fill the gaps:
   He washed his feet in the kitchen ________.
   The colour of his feet was ________.
   He had a long ________ from the mug.
3. Write five more words that rhyme with 'drink'.

Unit 14

FOCUS › '–ng' words

1 Copy the piece of string into your book. Write the '–ng' words inside the string.

string	this
make	gang
neck	sing
strong	king
long	race

The –ng string

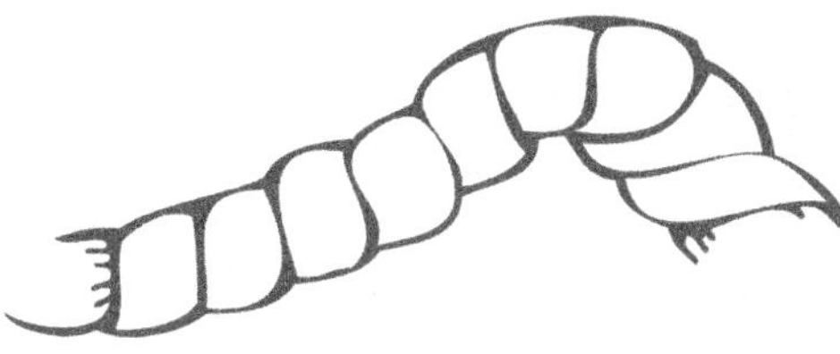

bang	plant
them	wing
hard	gong
thing	hung
song	what

2 Find the words for the pictures in the Word List. Write the words in your book.

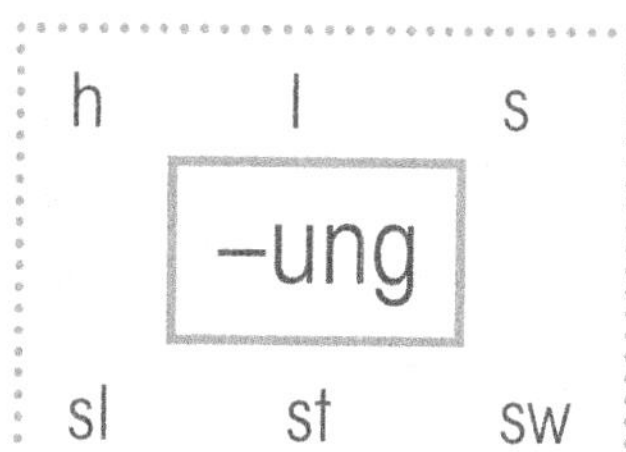

3 Use the '–ung' box to write '–ung' words in your book.

h	l	s
	–ung	
sl	st	sw

RHYME time › Copy this rhyme into your book and then ...

Ding dong bell,
Pussy's in the well...

1. Circle the '**–ing**' word.
2. Draw a square around the '**–ong**' word.
3. Finish the rhyme with your own words.

Word LIST

bang
fang
gang
hang
rang
sang
clang
slang
king
ring
sing
wing
bring
sling
spring
sting
string
swing
thing
bong
dong
gong
long
song
strong
hung
lung
rung
sung
slung
stung
swung

4 Use the '**–ing**' and '**–ong**' bells to write '**–ing**' and '**–ong**' words in your book.

s _ _ _

r _ _ _

k _ _ _

sl _ _ _

l _ _ _

s _ _ _

str _ _ _

g _ _ _

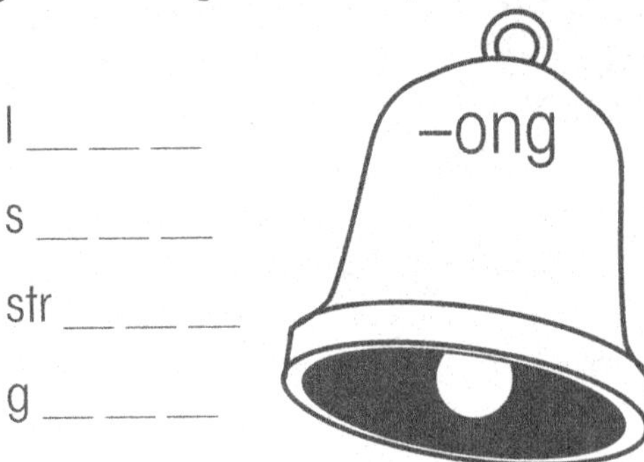

5 Copy this table into your book. Write the words from the Word Bank in the correct box.

–ang	**–ing**	**–ong**	**–ung**
______	______	______	______

Word BANK

rang lung slang thing bring sung wing bang strong wrong stung swing long dong sling swung clang gang

6 Use words from the Word Bank to fill the gaps. Write the complete sentences in your book.

a. The monkey has a _ _ _ _ tail.

b. The firecracker went off with a _ _ _ _ .

c. The _ _ _ _ _ _ girl lifted the heavy stone.

d. The bird's _ _ _ _ was broken.

e. She was _ _ _ _ _ by a bee.

f. Can you _ _ _ _ _ the book to me?

7 Choose the correct word. Write the complete sentences in your book.

a. We will (swing / sing) the song for his birthday.

b. It is (wrong / strong) to steal money.

c. She had her broken arm in a (sing / sling).

d. The (gang / gong) robbed the bank.

e. The gate shut with a (dong / clang).

WORD KNOWLEDGE > Proper nouns

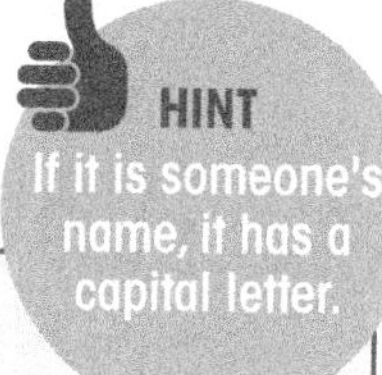

RULE

Proper nouns are special nouns that start with capital letters.
The names of people and places are proper nouns.
For example: *Michael Somare, Oro, Papua New Guinea.*

1 Write these words into your book.

a. Your first name and last name.
b. The first name of your mother or father.
c. The last name of your parents.
d. The first and last name of your best friend.
e. The name of your country.
f. The capital city of your country.

2 Copy these tables into your books. Fill the gaps. Don't forget to use capital letters.

Monday	Tuesday	Wednesday		Friday	Saturday	

January	February		April	May	
July		September	October		December

COMMON WORDS >

Choose words from the Spelling List to fill the gaps.
Write the complete sentences in your book.

1. Can we __ __ to the pictures tomorrow?
2. I come __ __ __ __ Papua New Guinea.
3. I have __ __ fruit for lunch today.
4. We __ __ __ __ to see the teacher.
5. They have to __ __ their homework.

Spelling LIST

go
came
from
no
do
sing
gang
lung
swing
long

RHYME time > Copy this rhyme into your book and then ...

On the Ning Nang Nong
Where the cows go BONG
And the monkeys all go BOO!
There's a Nang Nong Ning
Where the trees go PING
And the teapots jibber-jabber-joo.
by Spike Milligan

1. Underline the '**–ing**' words in red.
2. Underline the '**–ong**' words in blue.
3. Circle all the '**–ang**' words.

Revision

FOCUS › '–nd' '–ck' '–nk' '–ng' words

1 Copy this table into your book.
Write the words from the Word List into the correct box.

–and	–end	–ond

2 Copy this table into your book.
Write the words from the Word List into the correct box.

–ack	–eck	–ick	–ock	–uck

3 Complete these sentences with '**–nd**' or '**–ck**' words from the Word List.

a. The duck swam in the p ___ ___ ___ .
b. The hen tried to p ___ ___ ___ the boy.
c. The big t ___ ___ ___ ___ crashed into the tree.
d. You have to be q ___ ___ ___ ___ to win the race.
e. "I will s ___ ___ ___ you outside," said the teacher.
f. She had a ___ ___ ___ ___ ___ eye after she fell over.

4 Write each of these words in a sentence in your book.

clock stand neck bend crack blond sick luck

Word LIST

lend
back
quick
send
bland
and
rock
neck
luck
truck
sand
tack
land
pond
stick
bend
stand
sack
sick
lick
brand
clock
fond
peck
cluck
wreck
wind
black
lend
tack
speck

5 Copy this table into your book.
Write the words from the Word List into the correct box.

–ank	–ink	–unk

6 Copy this table into your book.
Write the words from the Word List into the correct box.

–ang	–ing	–ong	–ung

7 Use words from the Word List to fill the gaps.
Write the complete sentences in your book.

a. Sap came out of the tree t _ _ _ _ _ .
b. He s _ _ _ the song very loudly.
c. Jai was thirsty so he had a d _ _ _ _ .
d. I want to t _ _ _ _ you for the present.
e. The g _ _ _ of robbers stole the money.
f. The door shut with a b _ _ _ .

8 Write each of these words in a sentence in your book.

tank song stink spring trunk rung gang

Word LIST

swing
drink
bunk
thing
gang
string
thank
spank
hung
clink
junk
rang
trunk
shrank
sang
plank
hunk
lung
stink
sung
blink
tank
stunk
clang
bong
bang
chunk
kink
slunk
blank
slung
long

FOCUS › '–st' words

Word BANK

pest crust test just dust lost west
rust nest must bust vest list

1 Copy this table into your book.
Write the words from the Word Bank into the correct box.
Which words do not belong in the table? Why?

–est	–ust

2 Find the words for the pictures in the Word List.
Write the words in your book.

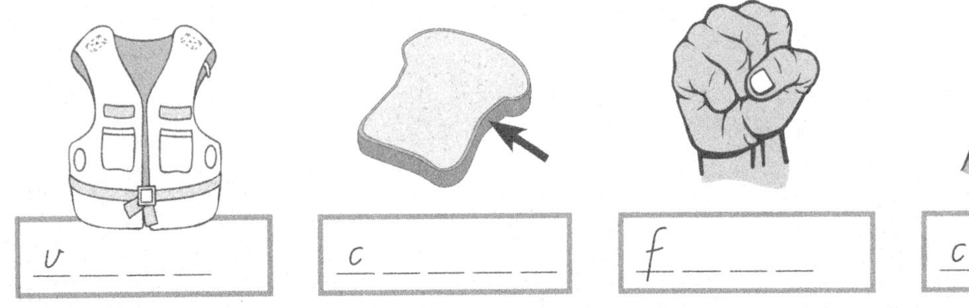

3 Use the '**–ost**' and '**–ist**' boxes to write '**–ost**' and '**–ist**' words in your book.

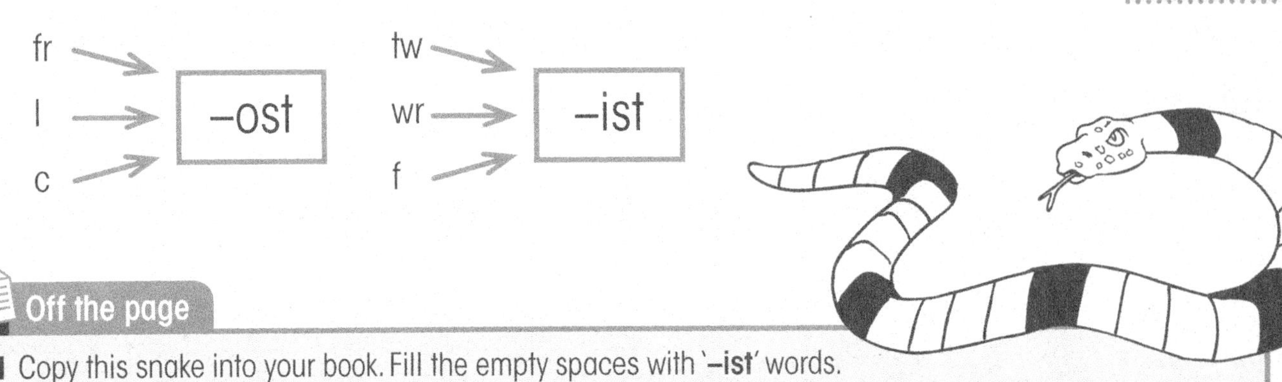

Off the page

■ Copy this snake into your book. Fill the empty spaces with '**–ist**' words.

Word LIST

nest
pest
rest
test
vest
west
chest
bust
dust
just
gust
must
rust
crust
trust
fist
list
mist
twist
wrist
cost
lost
frost

4 Copy the compass into your book.
Write 'north', 'south', 'east' and 'west' in the correct places.

5 Use words from the Word List to fill the gaps. Write the complete sentences in your book.

a. I saw three eggs in the _ _ _ _ .

b. My brother _ _ _ _ our ball.

c. The policeman wore a _ _ _ _ for protection.

d. The naughty boy was a _ _ _ _ in the classroom.

e. The _ _ _ _ _ on the bread was very hard to eat.

f. The _ _ _ _ of wind blew _ _ _ _ into our classroom.

6 Choose the correct word. Write the complete sentences in your book.

a. After lunch we will (rest / rust).

b. Dirty flies are a (test / pest).

c. The car was full of (dust / rust) holes.

d. The teacher wrote a (lost / list) of spelling words on the board.

e. The mountain was covered in (must / mist).

7 Find words from the Word List that have a similar meaning to these words.
Write the words in sentences in your book. The first one has been done for you.

an over jacket → *vest* *I wore a vest to school because it was cold.*

an exam paper →

a rush of wind →

a covering over bread →

a body part →

WORD KNOWLEDGE > Adjectives

RULE

Adjectives are describing words that tell more about nouns or pronouns.
For example, *dog* is a noun and *dirty* is an adjective – *dirty dog*.

ADJECTIVE BOX

fat
green
ripe
smelly
tall
hard
winding
angry
exotic
large

1 Choose an adjective from the Adjective Box for each noun.
Write them in your book.

____________ tree	____________ flower
____________ road	____________ pawpaw
____________ banana	____________ coconut
____________ fish	____________ cat
____________ pig	____________ village

2 Write two adjectives to describe these nouns.
The first one has been done for you.

garden → *large, overgrown*
sky → ____________
school → ____________
volcano → ____________
canoe → ____________

COMMON WORDS >

Spelling LIST

came
dad
mum
family
on
just
chest
lost
list
twist

Choose words from the Spelling List to fill the gaps.
Write the complete sentences in your book.

1. My _ _ _ _ _ _ lives in a village.
2. I go fishing with my _ _ _ .
3. My brother likes to cook with my _ _ _ .
4. My cat sleeps _ _ my bed.
5. My teacher _ _ _ _ to my house for tea.

Writing activity

■ Write about your favourite animal or pet. Write about what it looks like, what it eats and how it behaves. Don't forget to use plenty of adjectives in your writing.

FOCUS › '–mp' words

Word BANK

camp dump lump ramp limp stump
jump clamp pump bump stamp romp

1 Copy this table into your book.
Write words from the Word Bank into the correct box.
Which words do not belong in the table? Why?

–ump	–amp

2 Find the words for the pictures in the Word Bank. Write the words in your book.

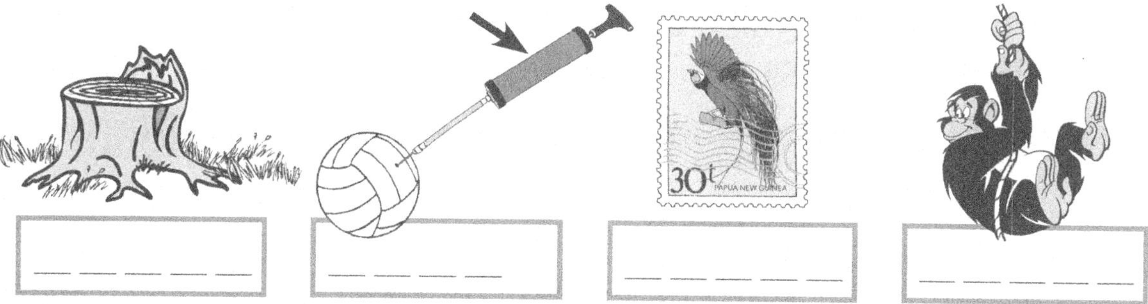

3 Use the '**–omp**' and '**–ump**' boxes to write '**–omp**' and '**–ump**' words in your book.

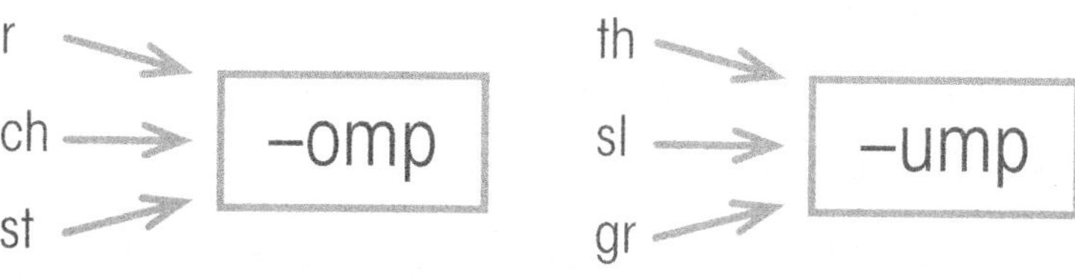

Off the page

- How far can you jump? Draw a line in the dirt. Stand with your two feet together and jump as far as you can. Measure the distance between the line and where you landed. Have a class competition. Who can jump the furthest?

Word LIST

bump
dump
hump
jump
pump
rump
grump
plump
slump
stump
thump
camp
damp
ramp
champ
clamp
cramp
scamp
stamp
limp
chimp
romp
chomp
stomp

4 Use words from the Word List to fill the gaps. Write the complete sentences in your book.

a. We make a ______ fire every night in our village.

b. The camel has a large _____.

c. The ______ escaped from the circus.

d. The tree ______ was very hard to remove.

e. Our classroom was very _____ because of the heavy rain.

f. I bought a ______ to put on my letter.

5 Choose the correct word. Write the complete sentences in your book.

a. The old man walks with a (lump / limp).

b. We love to (camp / cramp) in the forest.

c. I saw a cuscus (scamp / jump) up a tree.

d. My grandma is very (plump / grump).

e. My friends like to (chomp / champ) on sugar cane.

6 Find words from the Word List that have a similar meaning to these words. Write the words in sentences in your book. The first one has been done for you.

a bump on a camel's back → *hump* *The camel has a hump on his back.*

to leap in the air →

a kind of monkey →

a place where you put rubbish →

RHYME time › Copy this rhyme into your book and then ...

Bumpetty, bumpetty, bump.
Two elephants jumped on the stump.
The roos from the camp
Ran straight up the ramp.
Jumpetty, jumpetty, jump.

1. Circle all the words ending in '**–ump**'.
2. Draw a square around the words ending in '**–amp**'.
3. Discuss words such as 'bumpetty' and 'jumpetty'.

WORD KNOWLEDGE > Adjectives

RULE

Remember that **adjectives** are words that describe nouns.

1 Find adjectives from the Adjective Box to fill the gaps in this story.
Write the adjectives in your book.

Adjective BOX

village green rocky fishing rough spotted great

The v_______ children went on a f_______ trip. They visited a r_______ island. The r_______ island was surrounded by r_______ water. In the water they saw s_______ fish. The s_______ fish were feeding on g_______ seaweed. The v_______ children had a g_______ time.

2 Write two adjectives to describe each object.

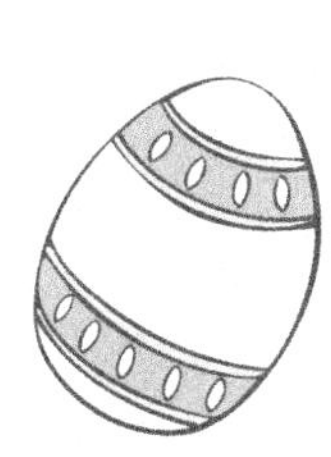

Weekly Spelling List to be tested at the end of the week

COMMON WORDS > Common words

Choose words from the Spelling List to fill the gaps.
Write the complete sentences in your book.

1. My village is a long way _ _ _ _ the main highway.
2. I _ _ _ a pet dog but he ran away.
3. We _ _ _ _ kaukau for dinner every night.
4. My brother _ _ _ a pet cuscus in a cage.
5. Our class _ _ _ _ to visit the market to buy peanuts.

Spelling LIST

from
had
has
have
went
stamp
jump
pump
camp
damp

Unit 18

FOCUS > '–sh' words

Word BANK

cash dish bash mash fish wish crush smash swish rush

Word LIST

ash
bash
cash
dash
gash
lash
mash
trash
sash
brash
clash
crash
flash
smash
stash
trash
dish
fish
wish
swish
hush
mush
rush
blush
brush
crush
flush
plush
slush
thrush

1 Copy this table into your book.
Write the words from the Word Bank into the correct box.
Which words do not belong in the table? Why?

–ash	–ish

2 Find words for the pictures from the Word List. Write the words in your book.

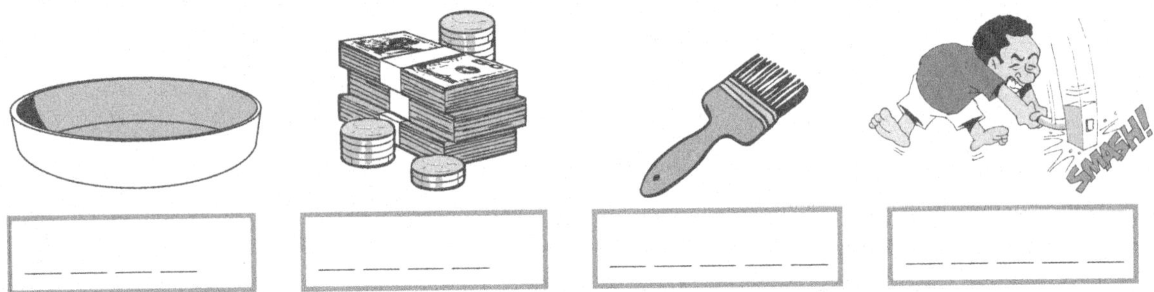

3 Use the '**–ash**' and '**–ush**' boxes to write '**–ash**' and '**–ush**' words in your book.

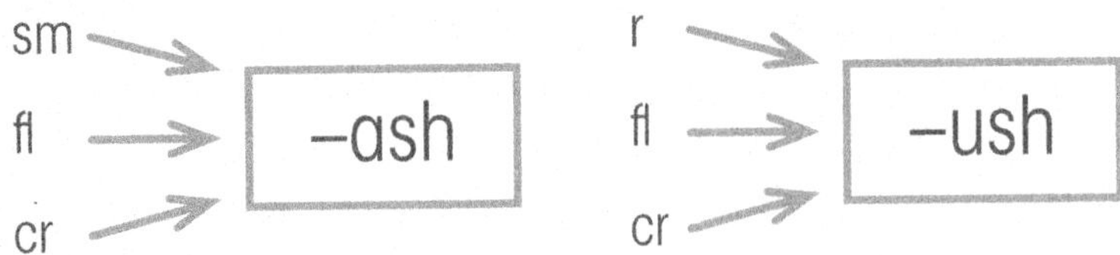

4 Choose two '**–ash**' words and two '**–ush**' words.
Write them sentences in your book.

5 Use words from the Word List to fill the gaps. Write the complete sentences in your book.

a. In our village, we like to eat ______.

b. We had to ______ to get to school on time.

c. The winner of the race received a red ______.

d. When the school bell rang to go home, we ran to the gate in a ______.

e. The businessman had a lot of ______ in his wallet.

f. I ______ I could go to town instead of working in the garden.

6 Choose the correct word. Write the complete sentences in your book.

a. We love to go the river to catch (swish / fish).

b. We need to (rush / hush) to school as we are late.

c. We need to (brush / blush) our teeth every night to keep them healthy.

d. My friend fell over and has a big (gash / mash) in his leg.

e. The men have to (lash / bash) the timber together to carry it out of the bush.

7 Find words from the Word List that have a similar meaning to these words.
Write the words in sentences in your book.
The first one has been done for you.

to tell someone to speak in a quiet voice → *hush "Hush," said the mother to the child.*

to be embarrassed, red in the face → ______

another word for money → ______

when cars have an accident → ______

RHYME time › Copy this rhyme into your book and then ...

Come over and splash in the water!
It's great to splosh in the wet.
Watch out for the splashes and splishes,
How much wetter can anyone get?

1. Draw a circle around the word ending in '**–ash**'.
2. Draw a square around the word ending in '**–osh**'.
3. Find the words with '**ash**' and '**ish**' in the middle.

WORD KNOWLEDGE > Singular and plural nouns

RULE

Singular nouns name **one** person, place, animal or thing, for example: a *boy*, a *tree*, a *house*.
Plural nouns name **more than one** person, place, animal or thing, for example: *boys, trees, houses*.

1 Make these nouns plural by adding 's'.
Write the plural words in your book.

tree flower road pawpaw banana cat pig village book teacher

2 Write these plural words in sentences in your book.

books pencils tables blackboards mats windows doors rulers chairs bells

COMMON WORDS > Common words

Choose words from the Spelling List to fill the gaps.
Write the complete sentences in your book.

1. My friend is __ __ tall as I am.
2. We will __ __ __ our teacher if we can go home early.
3. Our teacher brought a __ __ __ pawpaw to class.
4. We like to climb trees that grow __ __ the river.
5. The roof of our house is made __ __ sago palms.

Weekly Spelling List to be tested at the end of the week

Spelling LIST

as
ask
big
by
of
hush
crush
dash
mash
wish

Writing activity

- Draw a picture of a zoo.
Write plural word labels for all the animals, for example: lions, monkeys, elephants ...

FOCUS > '–nt' words

Word BANK

bent mint cent sent pant print hunt sprint spent hint

1 Copy this table into your book.
Write words from the Word Bank into the correct box.
Which words do not belong in the table? Why?

–int	–ent

2 Find words for the pictures in the Word List.
Write them in sentences in your book.

3 Use the '**–unt**' and '**–ant**' boxes to write '**–unt**' and '**–ant**' words in your book.

4 Choose two '**–unt**' words and two '**–ant**' words.
Write them in sentences in your book.

Word LIST

ant
pant
rant
chant
grant
slant
bent
cent
dent
lent
rent
sent
tent
vent
spent
pent
hint
mint
tint
glint
print
splint
sprint
stint
hunt
runt
blunt
grunt
stunt

5 Use words from the Word List to fill the gaps.
Write the sentences in your book.

a. Mum _ _ _ _ my brother to the store.

b. The doctor put a _ _ _ _ _ _ on my broken leg.

c. Did you hear that _ _ _ _ _ the village pig made?

d. The village elder taught us how to _ _ _ _ in the bush.

e. The _ _ _ crawled slowly across the table.

f. My bush knife was very _ _ _ _ _.

6 Choose the correct word.
Write the complete sentences in your book.

a. I (lent / lint) my cousin my soccer ball.

b. Our school (vent / spent) school fee money to purchase school books.

c. My mum made (lint / mint) tea for my grandma.

d. The sign next to the road was on a very steep (slant / grant).

e. The (chant / rant) coming from the classroom was very loud.

7 Find words from the Word List that have a similar meaning to these words.
Write the words in sentences in your book. The first one has been done for you.

something to set a broken bone → *splint* *I had a splint on my broken arm.*

something that is crooked →

damage to a car or truck →

money you pay to live in a house →

Off the page

■ Copy the '**–nt**' stairs in your book. Fill in the missing letters. The first one has been done for you.

		i	n	t
	t	*i*	*n*	*t*
s	*t*	*i*	*n*	*t*

		a	n	t

		e	n	t

		u	n	t

WORD KNOWLEDGE > Plural nouns

RULE

Singular nouns refer to one thing. **Plural nouns** refer to more than one thing.
To form the plural for most nouns we add '**s**', for example: *ant – ants.*

1 Read this story. Copy the plural nouns into your book.
Write the singular noun for each plural noun.

Cars and trucks were travelling very quickly along the highway. Suddenly some village pigs came out of the bush and ran onto the highway. Drivers slammed on their brakes to avoid the pigs. Men and women came out of the bush to see what had happened. Quickly the pigs were rounded up and taken back to their villages. Then the cars and trucks continued their journey.

2 Look at the tortoises. Write the answers to the questions in your book.
Use complete sentences with plural nouns.

a. How many tortoises?
b. How many legs?
c. How many shells?
d. How many eyes?

COMMON WORDS >

Choose words from the Spelling List to fill the gaps.
Write the complete sentences in your book.

1. _ _ _ spent her money at the trade store.
2. The teacher told _ _ _ to be quiet.
3. My sister played with _ _ _ dog down by the sportsground.
4. Dad caught some _ _ _ _ for our dinner.
5. _ _ likes to play rugby with his friends after school.

Spelling LIST

he
him
she
her
fish
chant
hunt
dent
spent
lent

Writing activity

- Imagine that you are going to stay out in a tent overnight and that you have to hunt for your food. Make a list of all the things you will need. Explain or draw pictures to show how you would hunt for your food.

Revision

FOCUS > '–st' '–mp' '–sh' '–nt' words

1 Copy this table into your book.
Write the words from the Word List into the correct box.

–est	–ist	–ost	–ust

2 Copy this table into your book.
Write the words from the Word List into the correct box.

–amp	–imp	–omp	–ump

3 Use words from the Word List to fill the gaps.
Write the complete sentences in your book.

a. The spelling l _ _ _ had ten words.
b. We will have a t _ _ _ for spelling tomorrow.
c. Please put a s _ _ _ _ on the envelope.
d. When he swept the floor the d _ _ _ went everywhere.
e. The children were l _ _ _ in the bush.

4 Write each of these words in a sentence in your book.

vest camp jump limp pump mist lost stamp

Word LIST

fist
bump
dust
test
camp
limp
chest
romp
twist
west
rest
rump
jump
chomp
just
lost
trust
champ
list
stamp
mist
gust
thump
stump
bust
dump
vest
cramp
cost
storm
must

5 Copy this table into your book.
Write the words from the Word List into the correct box.

–ash	–ish	–ush

6 Copy this table into your book.
Write the words from the Word List into the correct box.

–ant	–ent	–int	–unt

Word LIST

flash	dish
grunt	bent
rush	hush
smash	dent
hint	sash
pant	wish
fish	dash
cent	lent
crash	runt
swish	chant
ash	fish
stunt	glint
rent	trash
tint	sent
blush	print
grant	slant
crush	slush
sprint	hunt
cash	blunt
dint	spent

7 Use words from the Word List to fill the gaps.
Write the complete sentences in your book.

a. I saw the car s __ __ __ __ into the tree.

b. We went to h __ __ __ some wild animals.

c. The pig gave a g __ __ __ __ and then ate his food.

d. The cat lapped the milk from its d __ __ __.

e. We need some c __ __ __ to buy the present.

f. The slippery f __ __ __ swam through the water.

g. We s __ __ __ __ too much money.

h. The car had a d __ __ __ in the bonnet.

8 Write each of these words in a sentence in your book.

fish crash slush print grunt ant swish bent

Unit 21

FOCUS › '–ll' words

1 Sort these words into word families.
Write them in your book.

doll bell fell smell bill chill troll toll well pill hill roll yell

2 Find words from the Word List to match the pictures.
Write the words in your book.

3 Use the '–ell' and '–ill' boxes to write '–ell' and '–ill' words in your book.

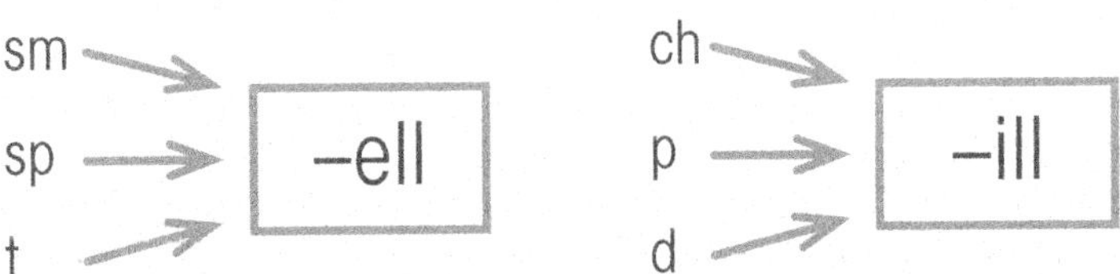

RHYME time › Copy these rhymes into your book and then …

1. Circle all the '–**all**' words.
2. Draw a square around all the '–**ell**' words.
3. Write the last lines in your own words.

Jingle Bells,
Batman smells,
Robin flew away
Father Christmas
Burnt his whiskers …

Humpty Dumpty sat on a wall,
Humpty Dumpty had a great fall,
Humpty Dumpty broke his shell,
Poor old Humpty …

Word LIST

doll
roll
toll
stroll
troll
bell
dell
fell
tell
well
yell
shell
smell
spell
bill
dill
fill
hill
ill
mill
pill
till
will
chill

4 Use words from the Word List to fill the gaps.
Write the complete sentences in your book.

a. We found a large _ _ _ _ _ _ on the beach.
b. Otto _ _ _ _ _ off the tree and hurt his leg.
c. The women in the village had to get water from a _ _ _ _ _.
d. _ _ _ _ _ you come swimming with me today?
e. My mother made a rag _ _ _ _ _ for my baby sister.

5 Find words from the Word List that have a similar meaning to these words.
Write the words in sentences in your book. The first one has been done for you.

toy → *doll* *Mum bought a doll at the market for my baby sister.*

a waterhole →
action to use magical power →
a small medicinal object →
to make something cold →
an object that makes a ringing sound →
feeling sick →

6 Copy this table into your book. Write rhyming words from the Word List in the correct row.

stroll	toll			
yell	spell			
mill	till			
bell	smell			

7 Use letters from the Letter Box to fill the gaps. Write the complete words in your book.

Letter BOX

d b d f r t h p w tr str ch sp

__oll __oll __oll __ell __ell

__ill __ill __ill __oll __ell __ill

WORD KNOWLEDGE > Plural words

RULE

Most **plural** words are made by adding '**–s**' to the singular word, for example: *tree – trees*.
For nouns ending in '**s**', '**o**', '**ch**', '**sh**', '**x**' or '**z**', we often add '**–es**' to make the plural word.
For example: *church – churches, box – boxes.*

1 Make these singular nouns plural by adding '**–es**'. Write the plural words in your book. Choose three of the plural words and write them in sentences in your book.

fox tomato watch match wish echo mango class potato

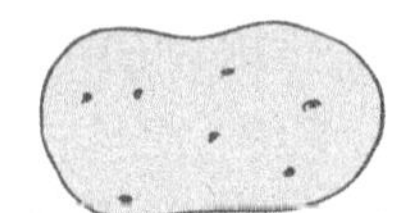

2 Read these singular words.
Write each one in its plural form in your book.

teacher brush desk glass dish town village cake class
table garden helper tax box flower hero volcano

3 Change these plural nouns into the singular form.
Write them in sentences in your book.

foxes pianos wishes schools matches

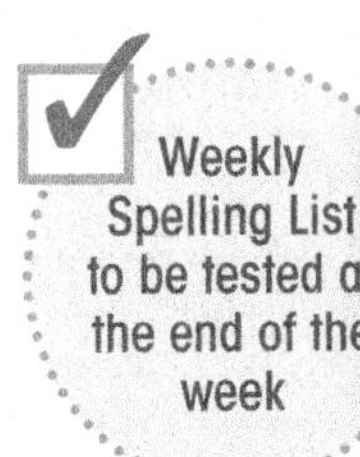

COMMON WORDS >

Choose words from the Spelling List to fill the gaps.
Write the complete sentences in your book.

1. Kaukau is a healthy _ _ _ _ to eat with fish.
2. The rotten fish had a bad _ _ _ _ _.
3. I told _ _ _ that our team would win the match.
4. _ _ _ _ you come with me to the game on Saturday?
5. _ _ _ I will come to the game with you on Saturday.

Spelling LIST

yes
you
will
good
food
well
smell
fill
roll
tell

Writing activity

■ Write about a time when you or one of your friends was lost at the market or in the bush.

FOCUS › '–rn' words

1 Sort these words into word families. Write them in your book.

barn fern corn worn burn thorn scorn
yarn turn horn morn darn stern sworn

2 Find words from the Word List to match the pictures.
Write the words in your book.

3 Use '**–orn**' and '**–urn**' boxes to write '**–orn**' and '**–urn**' words in your book.

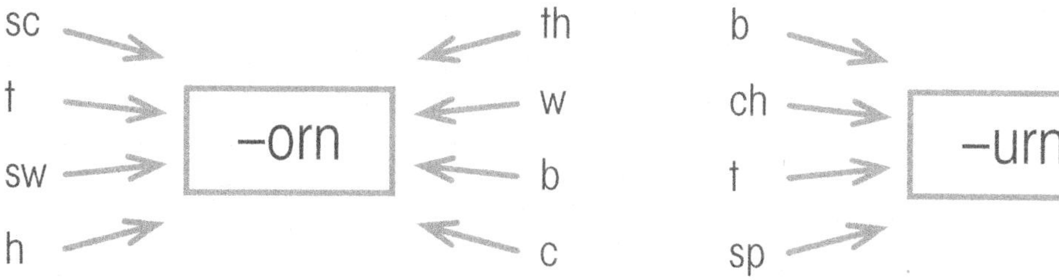

Word LIST

barn
yarn
darn
fern
tern
stern
born
corn
horn
morn
torn
worn
scorn
shorn
sworn
thorn
burn
turn
churn
spurn
urn

RHYME time › Copy this rhyme into your book and then ...

1. Circle all the '**–orn**' words.
2. Choose two of the '**–orn**' words and write each one in a sentence.

Little Boy Blue,
Come blow your horn.
There are cows to be milked
And sheep to be shorn.

Come back, Boy Blue!
Come blow your horn!
Come back to your sheep
And your cows in the corn.

4 Choose words from the Word List to fill the gaps.
Write the complete sentences in your book.

a. The baby girl was _ _ _ _ yesterday.

b. The boy's shirt was _ _ _ _.

c. The fire will _ _ _ _ until morning.

d. It is your _ _ _ _ to wash the pots.

e. The teacher had a very _ _ _ _ _ face.

f. It is so cold that I should have _ _ _ _ a coat today.

5 Copy these words into your book. Underline the letters that form rhyming patterns.
Circle the words that don't follow the rhyming pattern.

–orn

thorn born morn corn horn
bake sworn horn worn

–urn

burn turn churn
urn time spurn

6 Copy this table into your book. Write rhyming words from the Word List in the correct row.

corn	born			
fern	tern			
barn	darn			
churn	turn			

7 Use letters from the Letter Box to fill the gaps. Write the complete words in your book.

Letter BOX

d b d f m t h s sc w y c ch st w sw th

_arn	_ern	_urn	_orn	_orn	_arn
_orn	_ern	_orn	_ern	_orn	

WORD KNOWLEDGE › Unusual plural words

RULE

Remember that **one** 'thing' is **singular**, for example: one *boy*, one *coconut*.
Remember that **more than one** 'thing' is **plural**, for example: two *boys*, two *coconuts*.
Often we just add '**–s**' or '**–es**' to make a plural.
Sometimes there are unusual plurals, for example: *man* (singular) – *men* (plural).

Choose the correct plural words to fill the gaps.
Write the complete sentences in your book.

children men women people feet geese mice

1. There were 25 ________ at the school.
2. The _____ cackled when the fox came near.
3. The three ____ nibbled at the cheese.
4. The two _____ both had baby girls.
5. Dry your ____ when you have had a bath.
6. All the ___ in the village built the new house.
7. We saw ten ______ at the market today.

COMMON WORDS ›

Choose words from the Spelling List to fill the gaps.
Write the complete sentences in your book.

1. We went ____ the hut.
2. "Come over ____," said Mum.
3. Jon is _____ to the market today.
4. The ______ pig squealed loudly.
5. Our _____ is built on sticks.

Weekly Spelling List to be tested at the end of the week

Spelling LIST

going
house
into
little
here
worn
barn
fern
born
corn

Writing activity

- Write a list of all the things you do at a 'sing sing'.

FOCUS › '–tch' words

1 Sort these words into word families. Write them in your book.

match ditch fetch clutch itch catch sketch latch
wretch scratch patch stitch switch hatch witch hutch

2 Find words from the Word List to match the pictures.
Write the words in your book.

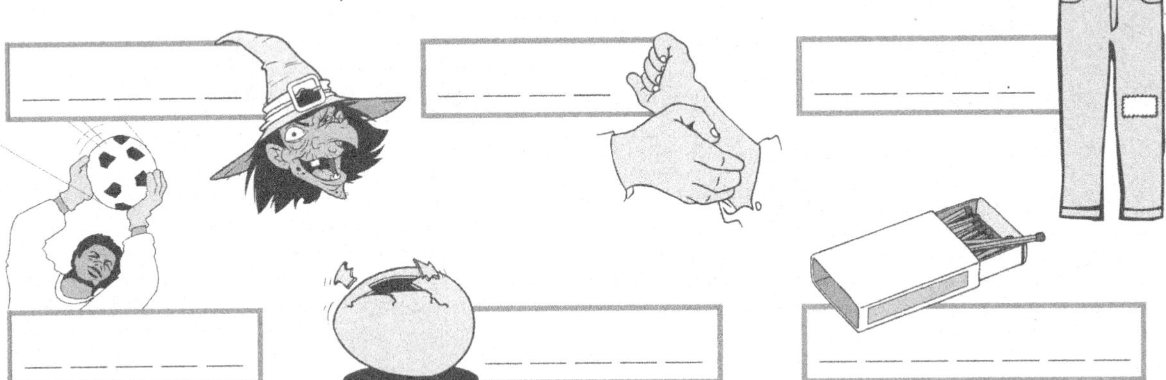

3 Use the '**–atch**' and '**–itch**' boxes to write '**–atch**' and '**–itch**' words in your book.

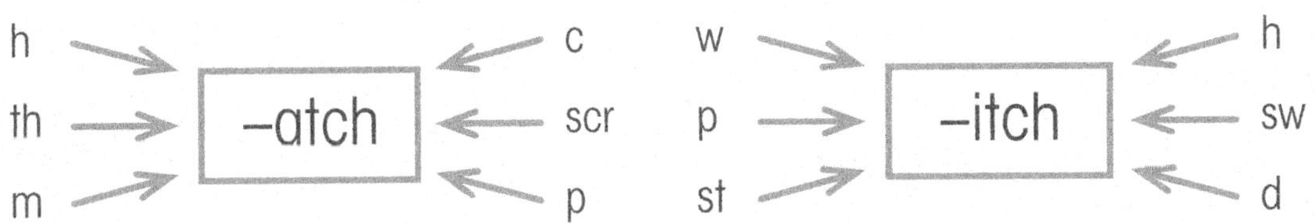

RHYME time › Copy this rhyme into your book and then ...

1. Copy the first lines of the other two rhymes and finish them with your own words.
2. Circle all the words that end with '**–tch**'.

Catch the ball one hand, *Catch the ball with two.* *If it slips through your hands* *Out go you!*	*Fetch the ball with one hand ...*	*Pitch the ball with one hand ...*

Word LIST

batch
catch
hatch
latch
match
matches
patch
scratch
thatch
etch
fetch
sketch
wretch
itch
ditch
hitch
pitch
witch
switch
stitch
botch
notch
blotch
crotch
hutch
clutch
crutch

4 Choose words from the Word List to fill the gaps.
Write the complete sentences in your book.

a. Can you _ _ _ _ _ the ball?

b. My shorts have a _ _ _ _ _ on them.

c. The _ _ _ _ _ has a pointy black hat.

d. We put the rabbit in the _ _ _ _ _.

5 Copy these words into your book.
Underline the letters that form rhyming patterns.
Circle the words that don't follow the rhyming pattern.

–itch

stitch ditch itch
hitch pitch switch
jump doll

–atch

latch scratch patch
learn hatch batch
catch snatch bike

6 Copy this table into your book.
Write rhyming words from the Word List in the correct row.

match	latch			
fetch	etch			
stitch	itch			
clutch	hutch			

7 Use letters from the Letter Box to fill the gaps.
Write the complete words in your book.

Letter BOX

d b l cl m h scr w p c sw

_atch	_itch	_otch	_utch	_itch
_atch	_atch	_atch	_itch	_utch

WORD KNOWLEDGE > Verbs

RULE

Verbs are **action** words. They tell you what someone or something is **doing**.
For example: monkeys *climb*, fish *swim*, babies *cry*.

1 Copy the action words in the Verb Box into your book. Add more action words of your own.

Verb BOX

sit walk jump cry swim climb stand hold drink cut eat

2 Use words from the Verb Box to fill the gaps. Write the complete sentences in your book.

a. The man _ _ _ the apple with his knife.

b. We _ _ _ _ to school every day.

c. See if you can _ _ _ _ over that log.

d. The fish will _ _ _ _ towards the worm.

e. Can you _ _ _ _ _ the tree?

3 Write these verbs in sentences in your book.

drink scrub stomp

Weekly Spelling List to be tested at the end of the week

COMMON WORDS >

Choose words from the Spelling List to fill the gaps.
Write the complete sentences in your book.

1. My dad will _ _ _ _ _ water from the river.
2. Do you know _ _ _ _ time it is?
3. I wake up early in the _ _ _ _ _ _ _.
4. The _ _ _ _ _ is very dark when there is no moon.
5. I will _ _ _ _ a necklace for my sister.

Spelling LIST

make
made
morning
night
what
hatch
fetch
ditch
blotch
clutch

Writing activity

- Write a sentence with the words 'scratch' and 'itch' in it.

Unit 24

FOCUS > '–le' words

1 Sort these words into word families. Write them in your book.

gale file hole mule male pale smile mole pole tile whale scale tale while sale role stole rule stale whole bale

2 Find words from the Word List to match the pictures. Write the words in your book.

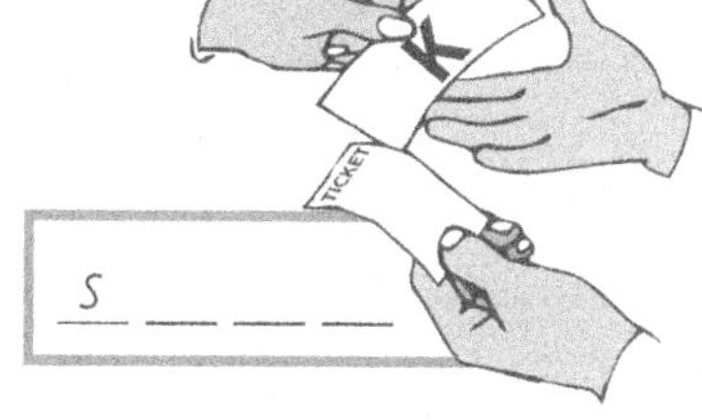

s _ _ _ _

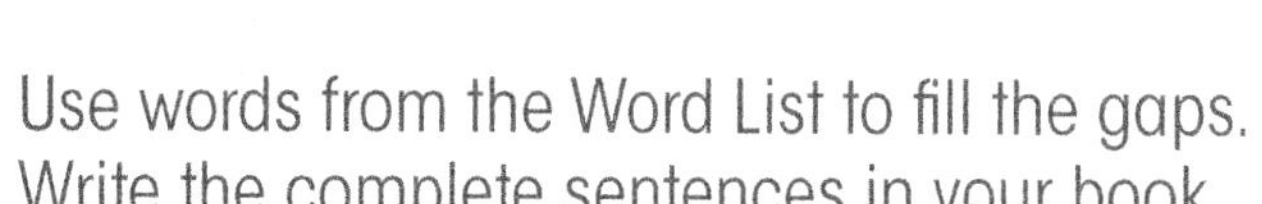

3 Use words from the Word List to fill the gaps. Write the complete sentences in your book.

a. I dug a _ _ _ _ in the sand.

b. The car crashed into the telephone _ _ _ _.

c. There was a _ _ _ _ _ swimming in the bay.

d. It is a _ _ _ _ that you must not hit someone.

e. The bread was so _ _ _ _ _ we could not eat it.

Word LIST

bale
dale
gale
male
pale
sale
scale
stale
tale
whale
file
mile
pile
smile
tile
vile
while
dole
hole
mole
pole
role
stole
whole
mule
rule
capsule

Off the page

- Draw a cartoon of yourself with a big smile. Write and complete this sentence underneath: I smile when ...

4 Use the magic word machines to make as many words as you can.

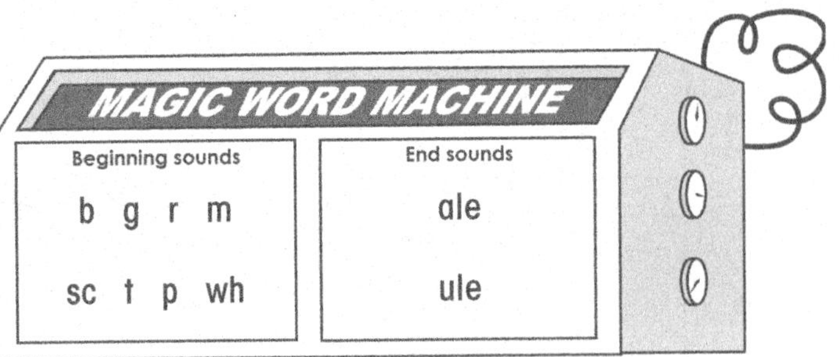

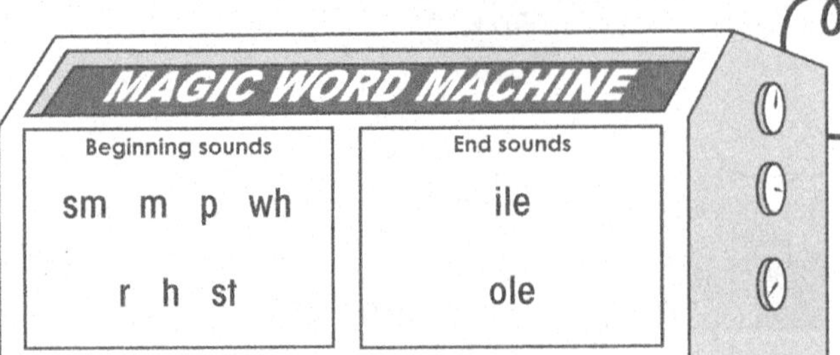

5 Copy these words into your book.
Underline the letters that form rhyming patterns.
Circle the words that don't follow the rhyming pattern.

–ale

scale male help dale
sale bale gale sell
stale tale whale

–ole

dole mole stole show
walk hole whole her
hole pole role

6 Copy these words into your book.
Circle the odd one out in each row.

mile	pile	stile	sale	while
whale	rule	pale	male	tale
hole	mole	stole	pole	pile

7 Use letters from the Letter Box to fill the gaps.
Write the words in your book.

Letter BOX

d b f d s h g m st r p sm wh

__ale	__ole	__ile	__ule	__ole	__ile
__ale	__ale	__ule	__ile	__ole	

WORD KNOWLEDGE > Verbs

✱ RULE

Remember that **verbs** are **action** words, for example: *walk, talk, eat, run.*

1 Copy the action words from the Verb Box into your book.
Place a tick next to the actions that you can do with your legs.

Verb BOX

scratch
run
stretch
skip
catch
walk
sock

2 Use words from the Verb Box to fill the gaps.
Write the complete sentences in your book.

a. I saw the dog _ _ _ after the cat.

b. Can you _ _ _ _ _ the ball?

c. We _ _ _ _ to the village.

d. When I have an itchy arm, I _ _ _ _ _ _ _ it.

e. I like to _ _ _ _ _ _ _ when I wake up.

3 Write these verbs in sentences in your book.

count shake crawl row shout

COMMON WORDS >

Choose words from the Spelling List to fill the gaps.
Write the complete sentences in your book.

1. Lae jumped _ _ _ the bridge.
2. Grandma _ _ _ _ _ _ with her grandson.
3. We _ _ _ _ _ _ everywhere for the baby.
4. The canoe was _ _ the middle of the river.
5. Let's do it _ _ _ more time.

Spelling LIST

looked
played
off
one
in
sale
file
stole
rule
pale

RHYME time > Copy this rhyme into your book and then ...

Circle all the words that end in '**–ile**'.

There was a crooked man and he walked a crooked mile. He found a crooked sixpence upon a crooked stile. He bought a crooked cat which caught a crooked mouse, and they all lived together in a little crooked house.

Revision

FOCUS › '–ll' '–rn' '–tch' '–le' words

1 Copy this table into your book.
Write words from the Word List in the correct box.

–oll	–ell	–ill
______	______	______
______	______	______

2 Copy this table into your book.
Write words from the Word List in the correct box.

–arn	–ern	–orn	–urn
______	______	______	______
______	______	______	______

3 Write these words in your own sentences in your book.

chill smell stroll shell spell thorn shorn churn

4 Choose words from the Word List to fill the gaps.
Write the complete sentences in your book.

a. Her old jeans were nearly _ _ _ _ out.

b. The fire started to _ _ _ _ the hut down.

c. Jack went up the _ _ _ _ to fetch some water.

d. We came to a _ _ _ _ in the road.

e. When the sheep were _ _ _ _ _ they looked cold.

5 Write each of these pairs of words in a sentence in your book.

will / spell darn / worn

Word LIST

chill
smell
torn
worn
toll
spurn
bill
darn
turn
churn
roll
hill
spell
burn
doll
yarn
stern
barn
horn
yell
stroll
dell
morn
shorn
well

6 Copy this table into your book.
Write the words from the Word List in the correct box.

–atch	–etch	–itch

7 Copy this table into your book.
Write the words from the Word List in the correct box.

–ale	–ile	–ole	–ule

8 Write these words in sentences in your book.

thatch stretch switch stitch wretch whale
stale scale smile whole stole

9 Use words from the Word Bank to fill the gaps.
Write the complete sentences in your book.

a. The egg in the nest began to _ _ _ _ _.
b. The strong _ _ _ _ blew all the trees over.
c. Her face went _ _ _ _ when she saw the witch.
d. The dog raced to _ _ _ _ _ the ball.
e. Michael's mum sewed a _ _ _ _ _ on his shorts.
f. The possum ran up the flag _ _ _ _.

10 Write each of these pairs of words in a sentence in your book.

scratch / itch hole / smile

Word LIST

catch
itch
mule
while
switch
scratch
pole
pale
match
stole
etch
hole
witch
tile
capsule
pitch
whale
hatch
latch
sale
file
gale
thatch
role
wretch
mole
batch
stale
rule
smile
patch

FOCUS › '–me' words

came
dame
fame
game
lame
name
same
tame
blame
frame
flame
shame
lime
mime
time
chime
crime
grime
prime
slime
dome
home
gnome

1 Sort these words into word families. Write them in your book.

came same lime flame crime home shame chime
dome grime game name tame mime slime

2 Choose three '**–ame**' words from the Word List. Write each one in a sentence in your book.

3 Find words from the Word List to match the pictures. Write the words in your book.

4 Use the '**–ome**' and '**–ime**' boxes to write '**–ome**' and '**–ime**' words in your book.

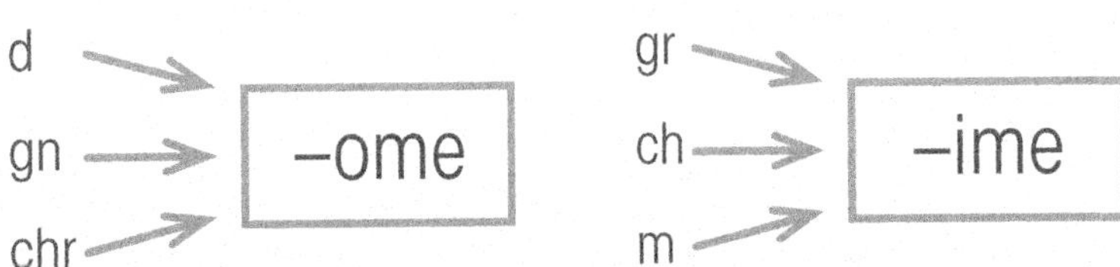

RHYME time › Copy this rhyme into your book and then ...

Circle all the words with the '**–ame**' rhyme.

I had a little brother,
His name was Tiny Tim.
I put him in the bath tub
To teach him how to swim.

He drank up all the water.
He ate up all the soap.
He died last night
With a bubble in his throat.

In came the doctor,
In came the nurse,
In came the lady
With the alligator purse.

'Dead,' said the doctor,
'Dead,' said the nurse,
'Dead,' said the lady
With the alligator purse.

Out came the doctor,
Out came the nurse,
Out came the lady
With the alligator purse.

5 Choose words from the Word List to fill the gaps.
Write the complete sentences in your book.

a. I wrote my __ __ __ __ on the front of my book.

b. At the bottom of the well was green __ __ __ __ __.

c. I put my family's photo in a picture __ __ __ __ __.

d. My teacher's __ __ __ __ is the __ __ __ __ as my mum's __ __ __ __.

e. Otto was sick at school so he went __ __ __ __.

6 Find words from the Word List that have a similar meaning to these words.
Write the words in sentences in your book.
The first one has been done for you.

can't walk properly → *lame* *After the race the horse was lame.*

a place where you live →

something that fits around a picture →

to act without words →

fire shaped like a tongue →

a kind of dwarf →

not wild or dangerous →

7 Copy this table into your book.
Write rhyming words from the Word List to complete it.

prime	time			
shame	tame			
chrome	dome			

8 Use these beginning sounds to write '**–ame**' or '**–ime**' words in sentences in your book.
The first one has been done for you.

ch *ime* → *The clock will chime every hour.*

sh

bl

gr

sl

WORD KNOWLEDGE > Past tense verbs

RULE

Past tense verbs are **action** words that have **already happened**. Many past tense verbs end in '**–ed**'.
For example: *talked, jumped, played, shouted, stayed, shopped, fixed, fished, hopped, pointed, cooked.*

1 Add '**–ed**' to the end of the these verbs.
Write the complete sentences in your book.

jump shout play fish

a. He ___________ in the classroom.

b. The horse ___________ over the hurdle.

c. We ___________ netball at school.

d. Dad and I ___________ in the river.

2 Write these past tense verbs in sentences in your book.

ticked washed looked walked

COMMON WORDS >

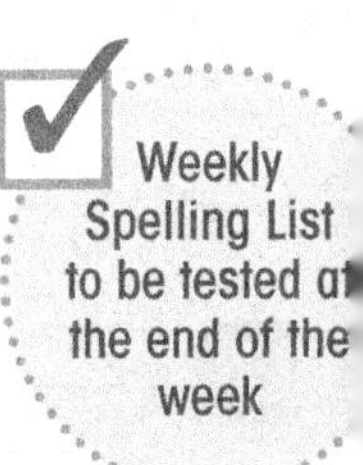

Choose words from the Spelling List to fill the gaps.
Write the complete sentences in your book.

1. Grandpa _____ a bird of paradise in the bush near our village.
2. A big lizard was sleeping _________ the house.
3. The policeman told _______ to go home.
4. The tree kangaroo was stuck in the _______.
5. The sing sing was cancelled ___________ it was raining.

Spelling LIST

saw
tree
them
under
because
shame
home
flame
crime
name

Writing activity

- How long does it take for you to get from school to home when you go the long way? How long does it take when you go the short way? Time your journey and write the times in your book.

FOCUS › '–ke' words

1 Sort these words into word families.
Write them in your book.

bake bike wake hike brake snake
woke cake like spike smoke fake

2 Choose three words from the Word List.
Write them in sentences in your book.

3 Find words from the Word List to match the pictures.
Write the words in your book.

4 Choose words from the Word List to fill the gaps.
Write the complete sentences in your book.

a. Our grade went for a _ _ _ _ in the bush.

b. My baby brother _ _ _ _ _ Mum's favourite cup.

c. The bus driver had to _ _ _ _ _ quickly to avoid an accident.

d. Mum will _ _ _ _ a _ _ _ _ for my party.

e. My friends and I _ _ _ _ to swim in the river every day after school.

Word LIST

bake
cake
drake
make
rake
take
wake
brake
drake
flake
snake
bike
dike
hike
like
pike
spike
joke
poke
woke
broke
smoke
spoke
stroke

Off the page

- Write your favourite joke on a piece of paper and give it to your teacher. The teacher can gather all the pages together, make a title page and staple them into a class joke book for everyone to read.

5 Use the '**–oke**' and '**–ake**' boxes to write '**–oke**' and '**–ake**' words in your book.

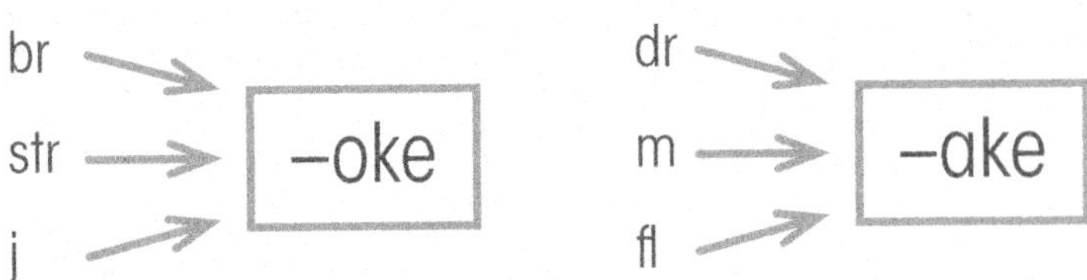

6 Find words from the Word List that have a similar meaning to these words.
Write the words in sentences in your book.
The first one has been done for you.

not real → *fake* *The man sold Dad a fake diamond ring.*

a male duck →

a two-wheel vehicle →

a funny story →

to finish sleeping →

a sweet food that is baked →

a poisonous animal →

7 Copy this table into your book.
Write rhyming words from the Word List to complete the table.

broke	stroke			
spike	pike			
flake	brake			

8 Use these beginning sounds to write '**–ake**', '**–oke**' or '**–ike**' words in sentences in your book.
The first one has been done for you.

sp *oke* → *Dad spoke to my teacher.*

h

sn

sm

sp

fl

WORD KNOWLEDGE › Irregular past tense verbs

RULE

Remember that **past tense verbs** are **action** words that have **already happened**.
Past tense verbs usually end with '**–ed**', but some don't follow this pattern – they are irregular, for example:
tell → told *see → saw* *do → did* *have → had* *cry → cried* *ride → rode*

1 Read these sentences. Change the present tense verb to a past tense verb. Write the present tense and past tense verbs in your book.

a. The village children have to walk to school every day.
b. We see many birds on our way to school.
c. The policemen ride on motorbikes in town.
d. Our teachers tell us not to be late for school.
e. Sometimes I cry when I am sad.

2 Write these irregular past tense verbs in sentences in your book.

told made sung run

COMMON WORDS ›

Choose words from the Spelling List to fill the gaps.
Write the complete sentences in your book.

1. We walk home _ _ _ _ _ the football match.
2. Grandma _ _ _ _ we had to tidy up the backyard before Mum comes home.
3. The _ _ _ _ of the new Province is Hela.
4. _ _ _ _ _ did you leave your jacket?
5. The new boy in our grade was _ _ _ _ quiet.

Weekly Spelling List to be tested at the end of the week

Spelling LIST

very
where
name
after
said
like
smoke
bike
snake
wake

RHYME time › Copy this rhyme into your book and then ...

1. Circle all the '**–ake**' words.
2. Draw a square around all the '**–oke**' words.

Billy Jean Drake
Made a mistake.
She lifted her foot
Right off the brake!

Jonathon Stoke
One morning awoke
And told his mum
A very bad joke.

For goodness sake,
Don't make that mistake!

FOCUS › '–ce' words

1 Sort these words into word families. Write them in your book.

space price spice lace race nice
twice place grace trace rice

2 Choose three words from the Word List.
Write them in sentences in your book.

3 Find words from the Word List to match the pictures.
Write the words in your book.

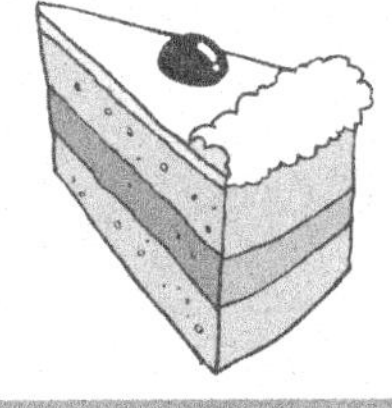

4 Make '**–ice**' and '**–ace**' words.
Write them in complete sentences in your book.

5 Choose the correct word. Write the complete sentences in your book.

a. Would you like a (splice / slice) of cake?
b. The (lice / mice) ate the cheese.
c. We need a (dice / price) to play the game.
d. It's not nice when you get head (mice / lice).
e. The astronaut flew into (splice / space).

Word LIST

face
lace
pace
race
brace
grace
place
space
trace
dice
ice
lice
mice
nice
rice
price
slice
spice
twice

RHYME time › Copy this rhyme into your book and then ...

Circle all the '**–ice**' words.

I have some rice.
I'd like some stew.
I need some mice,
What can I do?

Here's some mice,
And here's some stew.
Now add some rice,
And stir and chew!

6 Copy the word stairs into your book and fill in the missing words. The first one is done for you.

		i	c	e
	r	i	c	e
p	r	i	c	e

		a	c	e

7 Find words from the Word List that have a similar meaning to these words. Write the words in your book. The first one has been done for you.

frozen water → *ice* *During winter the water turned into ice.*

two times →

small white grains →

this makes food taste good →

moon and stars are in … →

the front of your head →

small animals →

8 Copy this table into your book.
Write rhyming words from the Word List in the correct row.

grace	trace		
spice	slice		
lace	race		
lice	ice		

9 Use these beginning sounds to write '**–ace**' or '**–ice**' words in sentences in your book. The first one has been done for you.

sp*ace* → *I would love to travel into space.*

sl

tw

n

gr

d

WORD KNOWLEDGE › Present tense verbs

✱ RULE

Present tense verbs are **action** words that are **happening now**.
Many present tense verbs end in '**–ing**', for example:
walk → walking *talk → talking* *fight → fighting*

1 Choose present tense verbs to fill the gaps. Write the complete sentences in your book.

walking singing jumping building working

a. The villagers are _ _ _ _ _ _ _ hard in the gardens.

b. The workmen are _ _ _ _ _ _ _ _ a new supermarket.

c. My friends and I are _ _ _ _ _ _ _ to the trade store.

d. _ _ _ _ _ _ _ is our favourite activity.

e. The frogs were _ _ _ _ _ _ _ out of the pond.

2 Write these present tense verbs in sentences in your book.

waking making playing

COMMON WORDS ›

Choose words from the Spelling List to fill the gaps.
Write the complete sentences in your book.

1. I walked home from the football match with my _ _ _ _ _ _ _.
2. My _ _ _ _ _ _ is older than my friend.
3. We like to go _ _ _ _ to the river every night for a swim.
4. _ _ _ _ is not my bag.
5. I will _ _ _ _ my sister a present.

Spelling LIST

brother
sister
down
this
give
race
price
lace
twice
face

Writing activity

■ Write quickly in your book for exactly five minutes. Write about anything that comes into your mind – how you are feeling, what kind of day it is, all about your pet – anything you like. When the five minutes are up, you must stop immediately.

FOCUS › '–ne' words

1 Sort these words into word families. Write them in your book.

mine tone shine pane lane lone pine phone nine plane bone

2 Choose three words from the Word List. Write them in sentences in your book.

3 Find words from the Word List to match the pictures.
Write the words in your book.

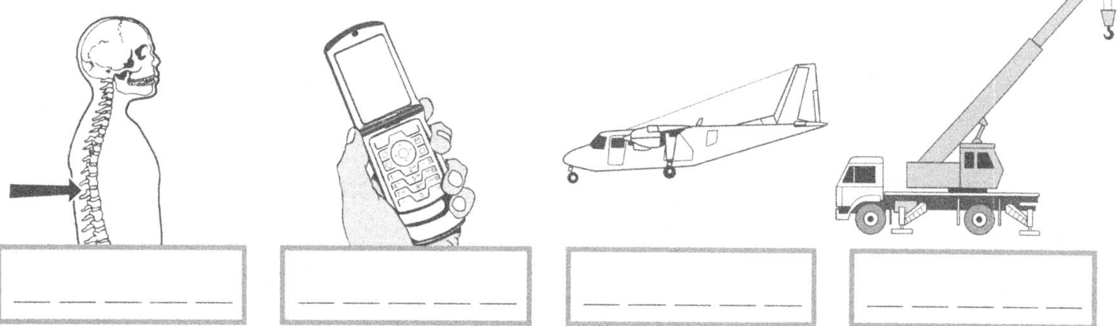

4 Use words from the Word List to fill the gaps.
Write the complete sentences in your book.

a. The horse has a white _ _ _ _.

b. Chai has a _ _ _ _ _ in his shoe.

c. I hope the weather is _ _ _ _ for the picnic.

d. The number that follows eight is _ _ _ _.

e. The _ _ _ _ _ lifted the car onto the boat.

Word LIST

dine	pane
fine	sane
line	vane
mine	wane
nine	crane
pine	plane
vine	Shane
wine	Dane
brine	drone
shrine	clone
spine	lone
swine	tone
twine	zone
whine	cone
shine	crone
bane	bone
cane	phone
lane	stone
mane	

Off the page

■ Copy the '**–ne**' word stairs into your book. Fill in the missing words. The first one has been done for you.

		i	n	e
	p	i	n	e
s	p	i	n	e

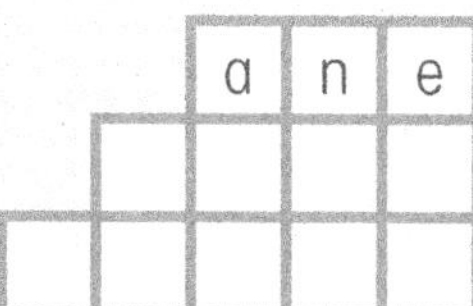

		o	n	e

5 Use the '**–ne**' boxes to write '**–ne**' words in your book.

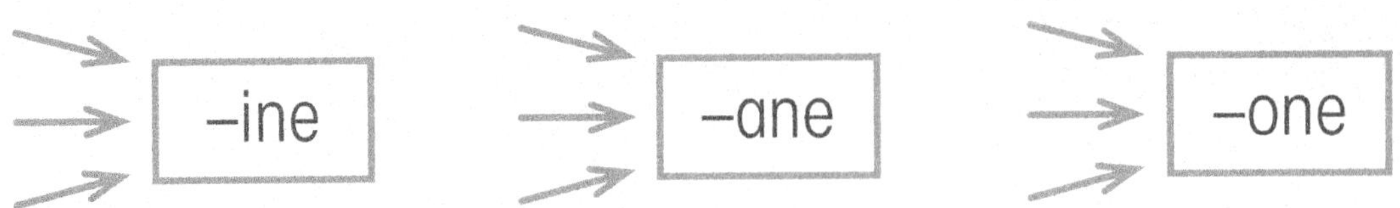

6 Find words from the Word List that have a similar meaning to these words.
Write the words in complete sentences in your book. The first one has been done for you.

to eat → *dine* *Last night we went to dine with my mum.*

your backbone →

3 x 3 = →

a small rock →

a kind of pig →

a flying machine →

7 Copy this table into your book. Write rhyming words from the Word List in the correct row.

dine	fine			
bane	cane			
drone	clone			
mine	nine			
mane	pane			
zone	bone			

8 Use the beginning sounds to write '**–ine**', '**–ane**' and '**–one**' words in sentences in your book.
The first one has been done for you.

cr *ane* → *The crane sat on top of the building.*

pl

sp

st

wh

sh

WORD KNOWLEDGE > Adverbs

RULE

Adverbs tell you '**how**' to do something.
They often end in '**–ly**' and are placed before or after the verb.
For example: *finally, really, slowly, quickly, loudly, neatly, quietly.*

1 Change the words in this box to adverbs by adding '**–ly**'. Write the words in your book.

tight careful neat
firm slow nice

2 Choose adverbs from this box to fill the gaps. Write the complete sentences in your book.

loudly quickly slowly
noisily quietly

a. The students sang the school song ____________.

b. The mice crept ____________.

c. The plane flew very ____________ into the sky.

d. The turtle walked very ____________.

e. The frogs in the pond were singing ____________.

COMMON WORDS >

Choose words from the Spelling List to fill the gaps.
Write the complete sentences in your book.

1. Jenny _ _ _ the quietest in class.
2. I walked _ _ _ _ _ _ _ to catch the bus.
3. The children sat _ _ _ _ _ _ _ in the classroom.
4. There were lots of _ _ _ _ _ _ at the match.
5. All the children _ _ _ _ basketball.

Spelling LIST

quickly
quietly
play
people
was
cane
wine
bone
lane
line

RHYME time > Copy this rhyme into your book and then ...

1. Circle all the '**–ine**' words.
2. Draw a square around the '**–one**' word.
3. Underline the '**–ane**' word.

Teddy Bear, Teddy Bear
Stand in line.
Teddy Bear, Teddy Bear
Count to nine.

Teddy Bear, Teddy Bear
Chew the bone.
Teddy Bear, Teddy Bear
All alone.

Teddy Bear, Teddy Bear
Catch the train.
Teddy Bear, Teddy Bear
Fly the plane.

Revision

FOCUS › '–me' '–ke' '–ce' '–ne' words

1 Copy this table into your book.
Write words from the Word List in the correct box.

–ame	–ime	–ome

2 Copy this table into your book.
Write words from the Word List in the correct box.

–ake	–ike	–oke

3 Write these words in sentences in your book.

smoke hike brake broke time name home shame

4 Use words from the Word List to fill the gaps.
Write the complete sentences in your book.

a. The teacher _ _ _ _ _ loudly to the boys in the class.

b. Her mother _ _ _ _ in the back door.

c. I go _ _ _ _ after school.

d. The _ _ _ _ _ from the fire was very thick.

e. The chocolate _ _ _ _ tasted delicious.

5 Write each of these pairs of words in a sentence in your book.

take / time came / home

Word LIST

came
bake
fame
bike
lame
hike
name
like
home
time
take
spike
chime
gnome
joke
tame
dome
stroke
cake
spoke
smoke
dame
lime
mime
grime
make
slime
brake
broke
shame

6 Copy this table into your book.
Write words from the Word List in the correct box.

–ace	–ice
____________	____________
____________	____________
____________	____________

7 Copy this table into your book.
Write words from the Word List in the correct box.

–ane	–ine	–one
____________	____________	____________
____________	____________	____________
____________	____________	____________
____________	____________	____________

8 Write these words in sentences in your book.

dine nice slice bore

9 Use words from the Word List to fill the gaps.
Write the complete sentences in your book.

a. The _ _ _ _ _ took off from the airport.

b. The _ _ _ _ ate the cheese in the trap.

c. She won the hundred metres _ _ _ _.

d. Three times three equals _ _ _ _.

e. She talked to her friend on the _ _ _ _ _.

f. All the children had to _ _ _ _ up in a row.

10 Write each of these pairs of words in a sentence in your book.

plane / place spine / bone

Word LIST

grace
clone
line
ice
phone
race
lice
fine
mice
space
tone
nice
lone
rice
pace
plane
dice
cone
lane
mine
nine
place
zone
slice
cane
mane
shine
spine
trace
sane
bone
lace

Unit 31

FOCUS › '–de' words

1 Choose the correct word. Write the complete sentences in your book.

a. The (bride / bide) wore a white dress.

b. The boy (rode / ride) his bike to school

c. The robber didn't know the (node / code) to the bank safe.

d. The man was very (crude / rude) to the girl at the supermarket.

e. The plane will (slide / glide) safely to the ground.

f. The (slide / tide) will come in late in the afternoon.

2 Find words from the Word List to match the pictures.
Write the words in sentences in your book.

3 Find two words from the Word List that rhyme with the words in the circles.
Write them in your book.

shade
made grade
fade

slide
wide hide tide
pride stride

Word LIST

bide
bride
chide
glide
hide
pride
ride
side
slide
stride
tide
wide
inside
outside
bade
blade
fade
grade
made
shade
grader
code
node
mode
ode
rode
strode
crude
nude
rude

4 Write as many words as you can with the magic word machine, for example: sl + i + de = slide.

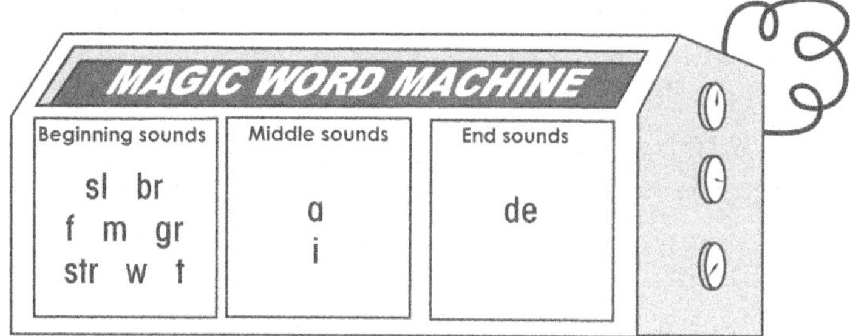

5 Find words from the Word List that have a similar meaning to these words. Write them in sentences in your book. The first one has been done for you.

a secret message → code The spy wrote a message in code.

part of bush knife → b

not in the sun, in the ... → s

wearing no clothes → n

not narrow → w

6 Use this code to find words from the Word List. Write the words in your book.

CODE:

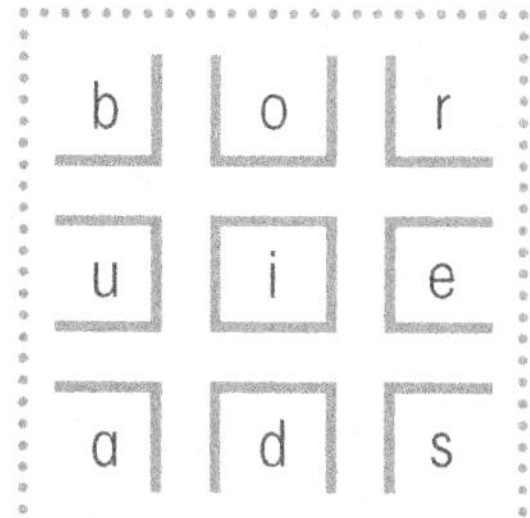

a.
b.
c.
d.
e.
f.
g.
h.

7 Use this code to write a secret message in your book.

a	b	c	d	e	f	g	h	i	j	k	l	m	n	o	p	q	r	s	t	u	v	w	x	y	z
1	2	3	4	5	6	7	8	9	10	11	12	13	14	15	16	17	18	19	20	21	22	23	24	25	26

When you have completed your own message, use the code to work out these messages. Write them in your book.

a. 8, 9, 4, 5; 20, 8, 5; 3, 1, 19, 8; 21, 14, 4, 5, 18; 20, 8, 5; 20, 18, 5, 5.

b. 23, 8, 5, 18, 5; 1, 18, 5; 25, 15, 21; 8, 9, 4, 9, 14, 7?

c. 5, 19, 3, 1, 16, 5; 14, 15, 23!

d. 25, 15, 21; 1, 18, 5; 2, 5, 9, 14, 7; 6, 15, 12, 12, 15, 23, 5, 4!

WORD KNOWLEDGE > Contractions

RULE

Contractions are **two** words that join to make **one** word.
We use an **apostrophe** to show where a letter is left out, for example:
it + is = it's, I + am = I'm, he + is = he's, we + are = we're.

1 Choose contractions from the Contraction Box to match the words below.
Write these contractions in sentences in your book. The first one has been done for you.

Contractions BOX

it's didn't he's can't I'm don't she's

a. it is → *it's* *It's going to rain tonight.*

b. I am →

c. do not →

d. he is →

e. she is →

f. can not →

g. did not →

COMMON WORDS >

Choose words from the Spelling List to fill the gaps.
Write the complete sentences in your book.

1. We _ _ _ _ _ like to work in the garden every day.
2. My friend _ _ _ a fishing rod.
3. _ _ _ _ a very hot day today.
4. _ _ _ going to visit my aunty after school.
5. My _ _ _ _ is a long way away.

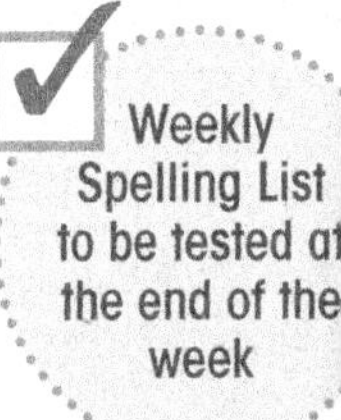

Spelling LIST

it's
I'm
home
has
don't
pride
made
code
rude
bride

RHYME time > Copy this rhyme into your book and then ...

1. Circle all the '**–ade**' words.
2. Draw a square around the '**–ide**' words.
3. Write about your own party. Who is coming? What presents would you like? What games will you play? What food will you eat?

Run and hide, slip and slide,
Cake to eat, open wide,
Lemonade, freshly made.
Now it's time to party!

Slip and slide, jump and ride,
Games to play, two a side.
Time to make a birthday cake,
Now it's time to party!

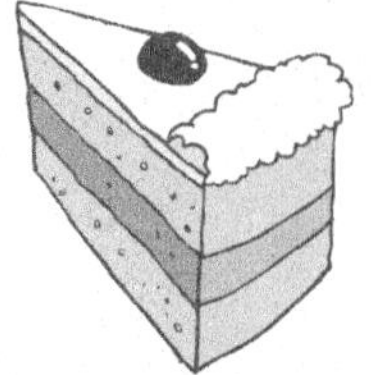

Unit 32

FOCUS > '–te' words

1 Choose the correct word. Write the complete sentences in your book.

a. My dad bought a (white / write) car.

b. The crocodile was put in a large (grate / crate).

c. The crocodile has an enormous (bite / mite).

d. The food was put on a big red (grate / plate).

e. We (date / ate) our food very quickly.

f. I will (write / white) a letter to the Post Courier.

2 Find words from the Word List to match the pictures. Write the words in sentences in your book.

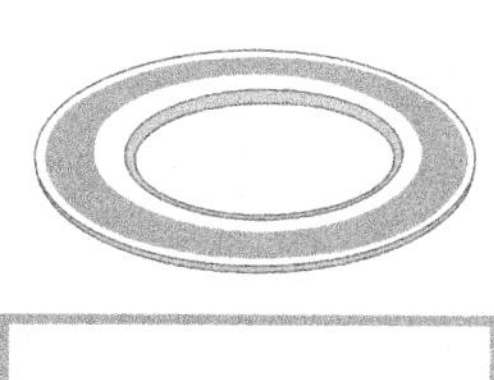

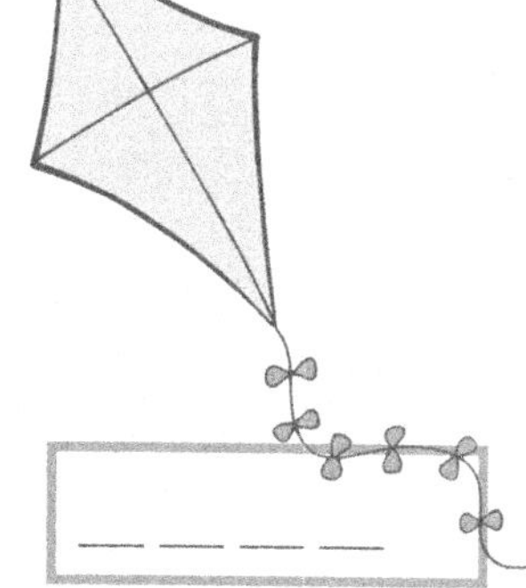

3 Find three more words from the Word List that rhyme with the words in the circle. Write them in your book.

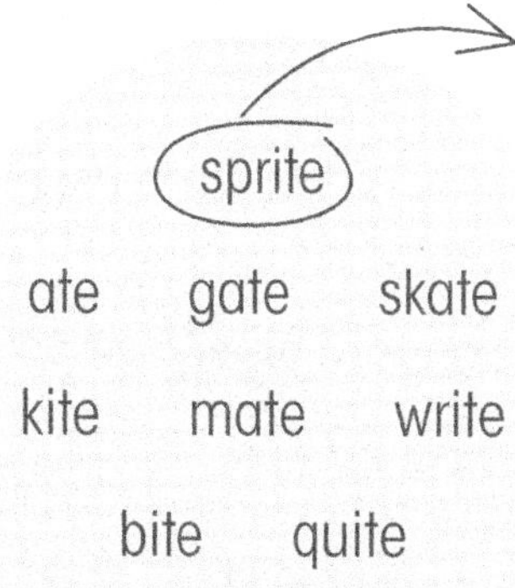

Word LIST

ate
date
fate
gate
hate
late
mate
rate
crate
grate
plate
skate
state
bite
kite
mite
quite
site
white
write
sprite

4 Write as many words as you can with the magic word machine, for example: gr + a + te = grate.

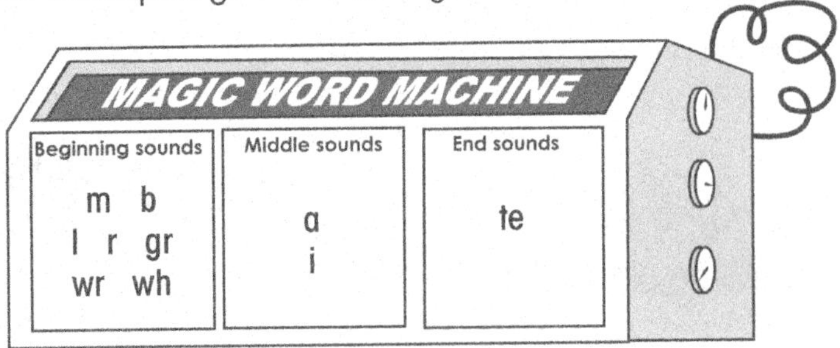

5 Find words from the Word List that have a similar meaning to these words. Write the words in sentences in your book. The first one has been done for you.

a male friend → *mate* *I went swimming with my mate.*

a light colour → *w*

to dislike → *h*

a large wooden box → *c*

not early → *l*

6 Use this code to find words from the Word List. Write the words in your book.

CODE:

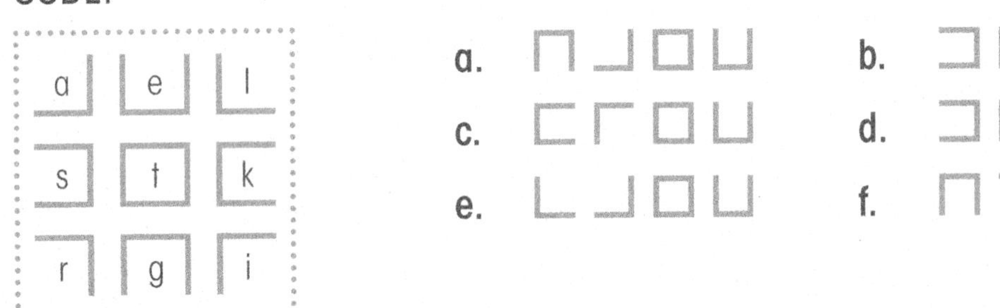

7 Use this code to write a secret message in your book.

a	b	c	d	e	f	g	h	i	j	k	l	m	n	o	p	q	r	s	t	u	v	w	x	y	z
26	25	24	23	22	21	20	19	18	17	16	15	14	13	12	11	10	9	8	7	6	5	4	3	2	1

When you have completed your own message, use the code to work out these messages. Write them in your book.

a. 4, 22; 4, 18, 15, 15; 14, 22, 22, 7; 2, 12, 6; 26, 7; 7, 19, 22; 20, 26, 7, 22.
b. 4, 19, 26, 7; 18, 8; 7, 19, 22; 8, 22, 24, 9, 22, 7; 24, 12, 23, 22?
c. 20, 22, 7; 19, 22, 9, 22; 10, 6, 18, 24, 16, 15, 2!
d. 18, 7; 18, 8; 7, 18, 14, 22; 7, 12; 20, 12.

WORD KNOWLEDGE > Contractions

✱ RULE

Remember that **contractions** are **two** words that join to make **one** word.
We use an **apostrophe** to show where a letter is left out.
For example: *don't, let's, I'm, we're.*

1 Write each row of contractions in your book.
Draw arrows between each contraction and the pair of words it matches.

he's	don't	let's	it's	she's	we're	can't	I'm
do not	let us	he is	can not	she is	it is	we are	I am

2 Change the words below into contractions.
Write the contractions in sentences in your book.

a. she + is
b. I + am
c. is + not
d. we + are
e. did + not
f. let + us

COMMON WORDS >

Choose words from the Spelling List to fill the gaps.
Write the complete sentences in your book.

1. The teacher was _ _ _ _ yesterday.
2. I will open the _ _ _ _ to get into the garden.
3. The _ _ _ man had to use a walking stick.
4. I will _ _ _ _ _ my name on the book.
5. The _ _ _ stopped when it ran out of petrol.

Spelling LIST

away
back
come
car
old
gate
kite
write
plate
state

Writing activity

- Write about a time when you were away from school.
  Some people stay away when they should be at school.
  Write why you think it is a good idea to be at school as often as you can.

FOCUS > '–y' words

Word LIST

bay
day
gay
hay
lay
may
pay
ray
say
way
bray
clay
play
pray
spray
stay
stray
sway
tray
boy
coy
joy
soy
toy
ploy

1 Choose the correct word. Write the complete sentences in your book.

a. The (bay / boy) went swimming instead of going to school.

b. Grandpa will (spray / stay) at home because he is sick.

c. The farmer dried the grass to make (tray / hay) for his pig's shelter.

d. The trees always (sway / stray) when the winds comes up.

e. We jumped for (soy / joy) when our team won the game.

f. The food was put on a (bray / tray) when it was cooked.

2 Find words from the Word List to match the pictures.
Write the words in sentences in your book.

3 Find three more words from the Word List that rhyme with the words in the circle. Write them in your book. The first one has been done for you.

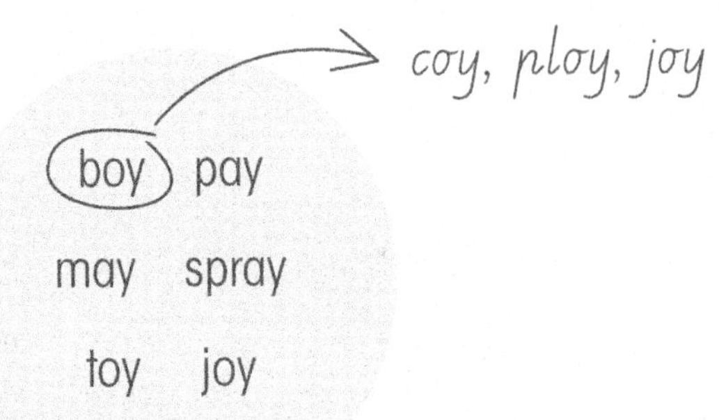

5 Write as many words as you can with the magic word machine, for example: sw + a + y = sway.

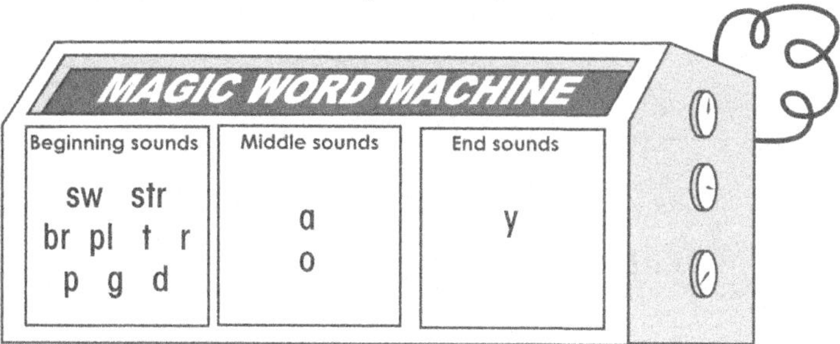

6 Find words from the Word List that have a similar meaning to these words. Write the words in sentences in your book. The first one has been done for you.

children play with it → *toy I gave my toy to a sick friend.*

a young male → *b*

the opposite to night → *d*

something to put food on → *t*

this is done in church → *p*

7 Copy these words into your book. Add a letter to make a new word. For example: way → *sway*

lay →

ray →

tray →

pray →

8 Copy this snake into your book. Write all the '**–ay**' words that you can think of into the snake.

RHYME time › Copy this rhyme into your book and then ...

Circle all the '**–ay**' words. How many did you find?

Anthony Hay,
On one holiday,
Thought he would go
For a swim in the bay.

A shark at play
Came that way.
Oh, what a shame —
poor Anthony Hay! (Sansom)

WORD KNOWLEDGE › Opposites

✱ RULE

Opposite words do not mean the **same** thing – they mean a totally **different** thing.
For example, *big* and *little* are opposites and *hot* and *cold* are opposites.

1 Copy these tables into your book.
Draw a line to connect each pair of opposite words.
The first one has been done for you.

up
hot
new
tall
boy
yes

cold
short
down
no
old
girl

2 Write the opposites of these words in sentences in your book.

hard long high young open rough

COMMON WORDS ›

Choose words from the Spelling List to fill the gaps.
Write the complete sentences in your book.

1. We read books ______ day at school.
2. My friend came ______ in the spelling test.
3. We need to ____ to the town by lunchtime.
4. The workers ____ paid last week.
5. It was _____ hot last Saturday.

Spelling LIS

every
first
get
got
very
day
spray
joy
boy
pay

Writing activity

- Draw a picture of two animals that are opposite in some way.
For example: an elephant and a mouse (big / little).
Then write a sentence for each animal to explain how they are different.

Unit 34

FOCUS › '–at' words

Word LIST

beat
eat
feat
heat
meat
neat
peat
seat
bleat
cheat
pleat
treat
heat
boat
coat
goat
moat
oat
bloat
float
throat

1 Choose the correct word.
Write the complete sentences in your book.

a. Mum bought (meat / neat) at the market.

b. The boy's handwriting was very (seat / neat).

c. The farmer's (moat / goat) got out of the paddock.

d. My friend's (throat / bloat) was very sore.

e. The (heat / meat) from the fire was very strong.

f. There was a (moat / coat) around the castle.

2 Choose words from the Word List to match the pictures.
Write the words in sentences in your book.

Off the page

■ Copy this story into your book. Use words from the Word List to fill the gaps.

The Three Billy Goats Gruff

Once upon a time, there were three Billy G___ts Gruff. They wanted to cross the bridge across the m___t and e___ the green grass on the other side. But there was a hungry troll under the bridge who wanted to ___t them up. So the Billy G___ts Gruff found a b___t that would fl___t across the m___t. When they reached the other side, they happily ate the green grass and wagged their tails at the troll.

3 Find three words from the Word List that rhyme with the words in the circle. Write them in your book.

pleat
cheat feat

oat
throat float
goat

4 Write as many words as you can with the magic word machine, for example: s + ea + t = seat.

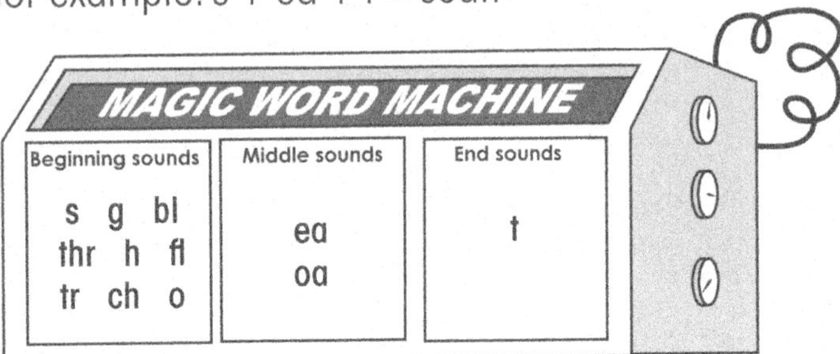

5 Find words from the Word List that have a similar meaning to these words. Write the words in sentences in your book. The first one has been done for you.

food from animals → *meat* *My favourite meat is chicken.*

very tidy → *n*

sound made by goat → *b*

it floats on water → *b*

something to sit on → *s*

6 Write '**oa**' or '**ea**' in the gaps to make words from the Word List.

f __ __ t h __ __ t c __ __ t ch __ __ t thr __ __ t
fl __ __ t s __ __ t g __ __ t tr __ __ t

WORD KNOWLEDGE › Connecting words

✱ RULE

Connecting words link one sentence with another.
Some examples of connecting words are *first, then, next, after that* and *finally*.

1 Use connecting words to fill the gaps. Write the complete sentences in your book.

a. F_ _ _ _ I got up. T_ _ _ I got dressed.

b. N_ _ _ I had breakfast. A _ _ _ _ t_ _ _ I cleaned my teeth.

c. F_ _ _ _ _ _ I walked to school.

2 Use the connecting words in the Word Bank to fill the gaps. Write the words in your book.

Word BANK

next finally first then

a. _ _ _ _ _ an egg is laid on a leaf.

b. _ _ _ _ a caterpillar hatches out.

c. _ _ _ _ the caterpillar spins a cocoon

d. _ _ _ _ _ _ _ a butterfly is born.

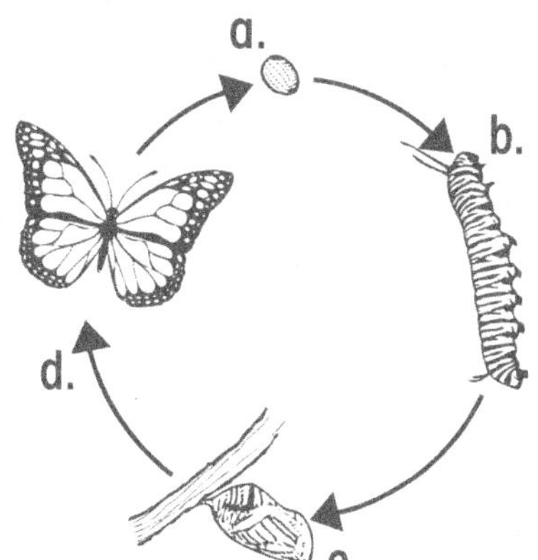

Weekly Spelling List to be tested at the end of the week

COMMON WORDS ›

Choose words from the Spelling List to fill the gaps.
Write the complete sentences in your book.

1. We all climbed _ _ _ _ the wall.
2. "_ _ _ your books away," said the teacher.
3. Dad will _ _ _ the drum oven.
4. Dad put _ _ _ _ petrol in his car.
5. There was only _ _ _ gorilla in the zoo.

Spelling LIST

over
one
put
some
fix
meat
cheat
boat
float
treat

Writing activity

■ Write down the steps you must follow to make a mumu.
Use the connecting words 'first', 'then', 'next' and 'finally' to begin your sentences.

Revision

FOCUS > '–de' '–te' '–y' '–at' words

1 Copy this table into your book.
Write words from the Word List into the correct box.

–ide	–ade	–ode

2 Copy this table into your book.
Write words from the Word List into the correct box.

–ate	–ite

3 Write these words in sentences in your book.

inside ride hide strode

4 Use words from the Word List to fill the gaps.
Write the complete sentences in your book.

a. I am going to _ _ _ _ _ a letter.

b. The _ _ _ _ _ on the knife is very sharp.

c. It took a long while for the fish to _ _ _ _.

d. When it is hot I like to sit in the _ _ _ _ _ of a coconut tree.

e. He _ _ _ _ a bike to school.

5 Write each of these pairs of words in a sentence in your book.

inside / outside black / white

Word LIST

bride
fade
ate
made
grate
hide
bite
kite
plate
tide
code
grade
white
state
date
ride
strode
blade
rude
rode
quite
mite
rate
slide
crude
site
write
inside
outside
shade

6 Copy this table into your book.
Write words from the Word List into the correct box.

–ay	–oy
____	____
____	____
____	____

7 Write these words in sentences of your own.

spray joy play boy

8 Copy this table into your book.
Write words from the Word List into the correct box.

–eat	–oat
____	____
____	____
____	____
____	____

9 Use words from the Word Bank to fill the gaps.
Write the complete sentences in your book.

a. The _ _ _ _ sank when it hit the rocks.

b. I have a sore _ _ _ _ _ _.

c. The girls like to _ _ _ _ outside at lunch time.

d. We found a _ _ _ _ _ cat under the house.

e. We watched the leaves _ _ _ _ _ on the water.

10 Write each of these pairs of words in a sentence in your book.

toy / boy may / play

Word LIST

beat
boy
boat
stray
sway
play
goat
heat
ray
coy
lay
float
may
joy
bleat
coat
tray
say
pray
toy
cheat
pleat
bloat
neat
way
bay
soy
throat
oat
spray
ploy

FOCUS > '–rk' words

1 Choose the correct word. Write the complete sentences in your book.

a. The dog's (lark / bark) is very loud.

b. The (stork / shark) circled around the boat.

c. I don't like going out when it is (bark / dark).

d. My teacher put a (mark / hark) on the map to show our destination.

e. A (cork / stork) is used to seal a bottle.

f. A (stork / stark) builds her nest high in trees.

Word LIST

bark
dark
hark
lark
mark
park
shark
spark
stark
cork
fork
pork
stork

2 Choose words for the pictures from the Word List.
Write the words in sentences in your book.

3 Find three words from the Word List that rhyme with the words in the circle.
Write them in your book.

stark
mark park

pork

4 Write as many words as you can with the magic word machine, for example: c + o + rk = cork.

MAGIC WORD MACHINE

Beginning sounds	Middle sounds	End sounds
c d m f sh st p sp	o a	rk

5 Find words from the Word List that have a similar meaning to these words. Write the words in sentences in your book. The first one has been done for you.

a bird that nests in a tree → *stork The stork lives in a nest high in the trees.*

an eating utensil → *f*

a man-eating fish → *sh*

meat from a pig → *p*

to make a noise like a dog → *b*

6 Use this code to find words from the Word List. Write the words in your book.

CODE:

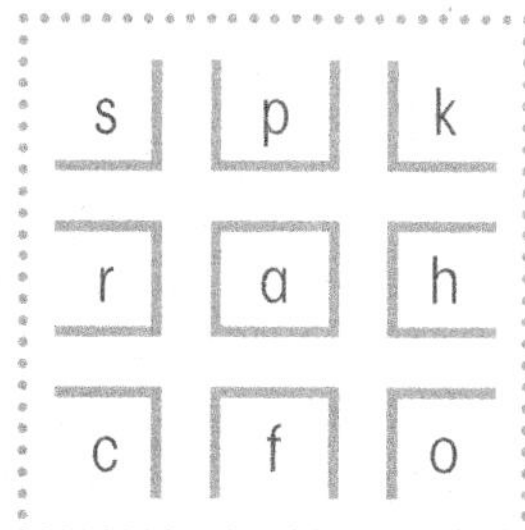

a.

b.

c.

d.

e.

f.

7 Use this code to write a secret message in your book.

a	b	c	d	e	f	g	h	i	j	k	l	m	n	o	p	q	r	s	t	u	v	w	x	y	z
1	2	3	4	5	6	7	8	9	10	11	12	13	14	15	16	17	18	19	20	21	22	23	24	25	26

When you have completed your own message, use the code to work out these messages. Write them in your book.

a. 13, 1, 18, 11; 20, 8, 5; 19, 16, 15, 20; 23, 9, 20, 8; 1, 14; 24.

b. 3, 15, 13, 5; 17, 21, 9, 3, 11, 12, 25!

c. 14, 5, 5, 4; 8, 5, 12, 16; 14, 15, 23!

d. 23, 8, 5, 14; 23, 9, 12, 12; 23, 5; 13, 5, 5, 20?

WORD KNOWLEDGE > Prefix 'un'

RULE

A **prefix** is a syllable attached to the **beginning** of a word. It changes the meaning of the word. For example, the prefix '**–un**' changes a word to mean the opposite (*tidy / untidy*).

1 Add the prefix '**–un**' to each of the words below to make a word with the opposite meaning. The first one has been done for you.

healthy → *unhealthy*	wise ______	safe ______
friendly ______	fit ______	sure ______
kind ______	happy ______	fair ______

2 Write these words in sentences in your book to show the difference in meaning.

tie untie

COMMON WORDS >

Choose words from the Spelling List to fill the gaps.
Write the complete sentences in your book.

1. The _ _ _ _ was closed.
2. People all have _ _ _ legs and _ _ _ arms.
3. I have _ _ _ _ _ brothers and _ _ _ sisters.
4. I bought _ _ _ _ bananas at the market.
5. We all have _ _ _ _ fingers on each hand.

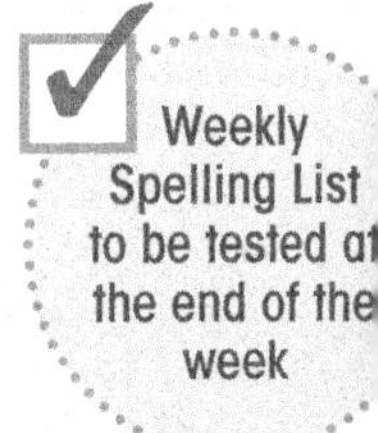

Spelling LIST

door
two
three
four
five
park
spark
stork
pork
fork

RHYME time > Copy this rhyme into your book and then ...

1. Circle all the '**–ark**' words. How many are there?
2. Finish the last line with your own words.

In a dark, dark wood
There was a dark, dark house.
In that dark, dark house
There was a dark, dark cupboard.
In that dark, dark cupboard
There was a dark, dark shelf.
On that dark, dark shelf
There was a dark, dark box,
And in that dark, dark box
There was a . . .

FOCUS › '–rt' words

Word LIST

cart
dart
part
tart
chart
smart
start
dirt
flirt
shirt
skirt
squirt
fort
port
sort
short
snort
sport
curt
hurt
spurt
blurt

1 Choose the correct word. Write the complete sentences in your book.

a. The girl wore a red (skirt / flirt).

b. At our school we play volleyball as a school (sort / sport).

c. My mum made a lemon (part / tart) for my party.

d. The ship sailed into (fort /port).

e. The girl wore a very (sort / short) skirt to school.

f. Grandpa makes a very loud (sort / snort) when he sleeps.

2 Find the words for the pictures in the Word List.
Write the words in sentences in your book.

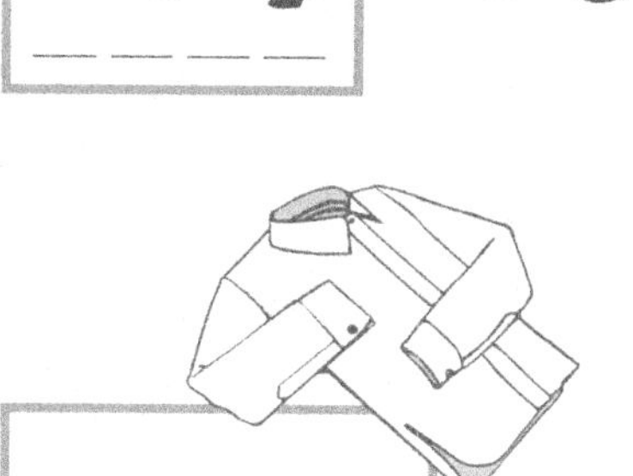

3 Find all the words in the Word List that start with '–sh', '–sp', '–ch' and '–bl'.
Write these words in sentences in your book.

RHYME time › Copy this rhyme into your book and then ...

1. Circle all the '**–irt**' words.
2. Draw a square around the '**–ert**' word.

I'm in the dirt,
So is my shirt.
I'm so dirty,
So is my shirty.
What a dirty shirt!

Gert's in the dirt,
So is her skirt.
She is dirty,
So is her skirt.
What a dirty Gert!

4 Copy these word grids into your book.
Change one letter in each grid to make a new word that matches the picture.

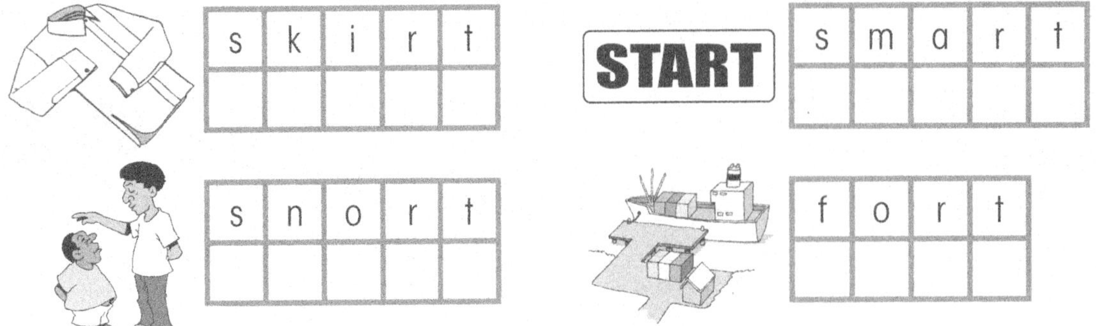

5 Write as many words as you can with the magic word machine,
for example: sk + i + rt = skirt.

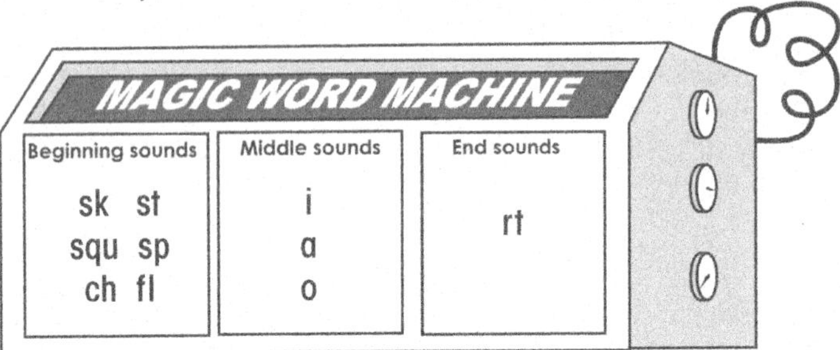

6 Find words from the Word List that have a similar meaning.
Write the words in sentences in your book.
The first one has been done for you.

not long → *short* *The girl's skirt was very short.*

a place where ships anchor → *p*

very clever → *sm*

a loud noise → *sn*

a kind of wheelbarrow → *c*

7 Write '**ar**', '**ir**', '**or**' or '**ur**' in the gaps to make words from the Word List.
Write the complete words in your book.

sh __ __ t	squ __ __ t	fl __ __ t	sp __ __ t
t __ __ t	d __ __ t	sn __ __ t	sk __ __ t

WORD KNOWLEDGE > Comparisons

RULE

Adding '**–er**' and/or '**–est**' to the end of a word helps us to compare things.
For example, Michael is big, Tom is bigg*er* and John is the bigg*est* of all!

1 Copy this table into your book.
Complete the rows with '**–er**' or '**–est**' words.

big	bigger	biggest
short	shorter	
quick		quickest
hard	harder	
tall		

2 Write sentences with these words in your book.

small smaller smallest

COMMON WORDS >

Choose words from the Spelling List to fill the gaps.
Write the complete sentences in your book.

1. The children took _ _ _ _ _ dog to school.
2. We had _ _ _ at the party.
3. We go swimming after _ _ _ _ _ _.
4. There was no _ _ _ _ on the PMV so we had to walk home.
5. The table was _ _ _ heavy to lift by ourselves.

Weekly Spelling List to be tested at the end of the week

Spelling LIST

too
their
school
room
fun
skirt
smart
sport
start
port

Writing activity

- What is the smallest animal that you can think of?
  What is the largest?
  Draw a picture of both animals and add labels.
  Write a sentence about each one.

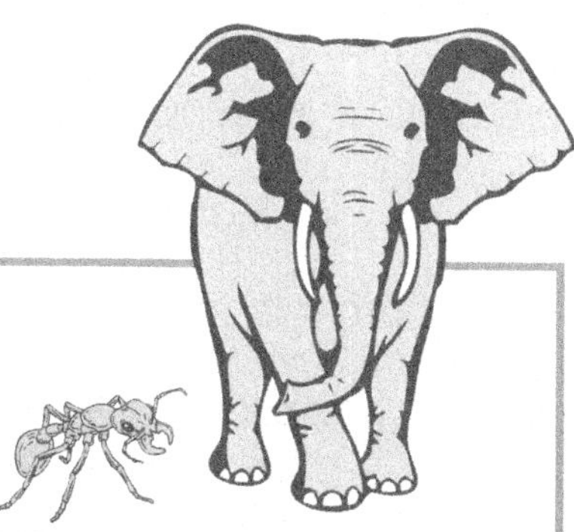

Unit 38

FOCUS › '–il' words

1 Choose the correct word. Write the complete sentences in your book.

a. The cuscus has a long (trail / tail).

b. The yacht has a large, white (hail / sail).

c. All car engines need (coil / oil).

d. We plant vegetables in (soil / sail).

e. We (foil / boil) water to make it safe to drink.

f. My grandma is very (mail / frail).

2 Choose words for the pictures from the Word List.
Write the words in sentences in your book.

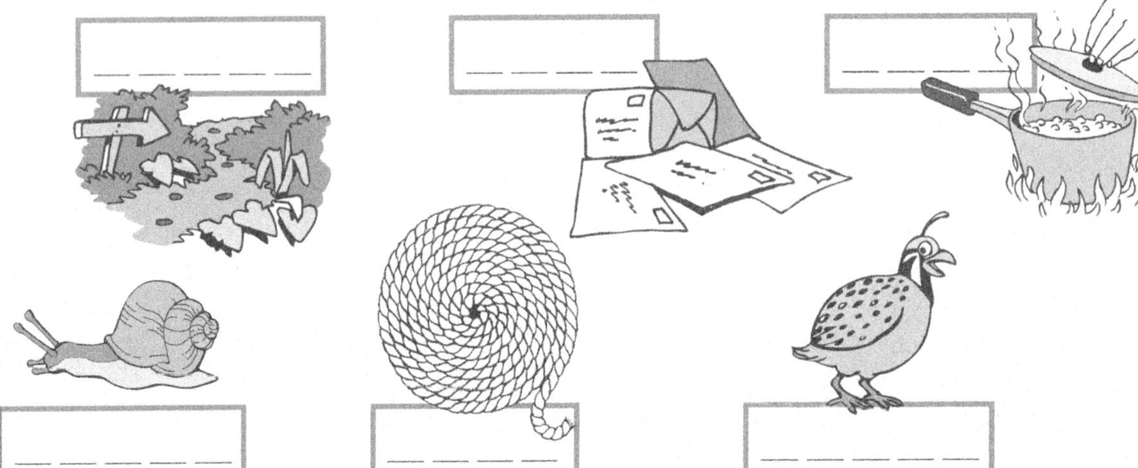

3 Choose words from the Word List to fill the gaps.
Write the complete sentences in your book.

a. The _ _ _ _ _ leaves a slime t _ _ _ _ .

b. Dad used a hammer to bang in the _ _ _ _.

c. The old woman was very _ _ _ _ _.

d. Mum stood on the cat's _ _ _ _.

Word LIST

bail
fail
hail
jail
mail
nail
pail
quail
rail
sail
tail
wail
frail
snail
trail
boil
coil
foil
oil
soil
toil
spoil
broil

4 Copy these word grids into your book.
Change one letter in each grid to make a new word that matches the picture.

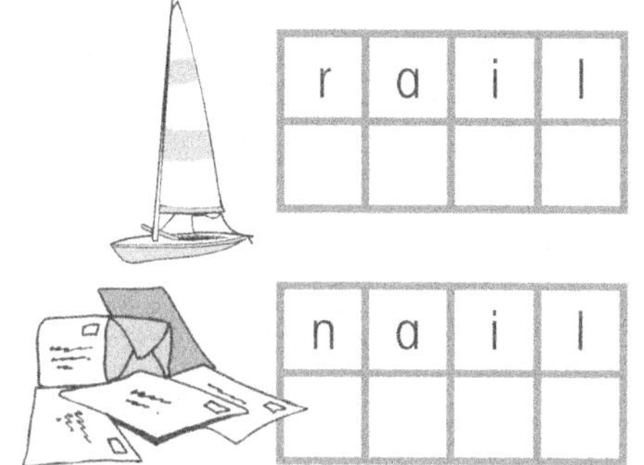

n	a	i	l

s	o	i	l

5 Write as many words as you can with the magic word machine,
for example: qu + a +il = quail.

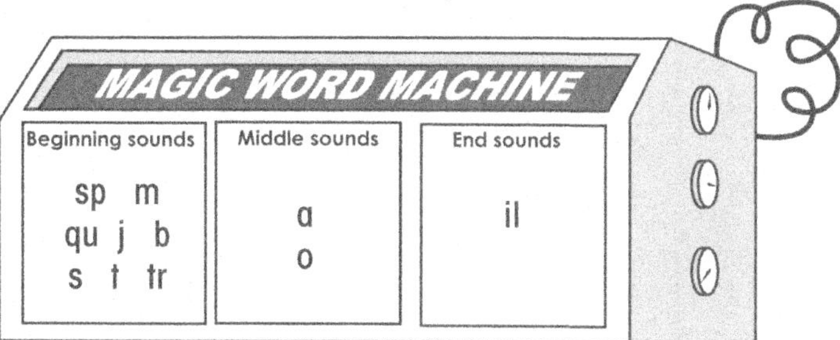

6 Find words from the Word List that have a similar meaning.
Write the words in sentences in your book. The first one has been done for you.

to work hard → *toil* *The villages toil in their gardens everyday.*

very weak → *fr*

where bad people are locked up → *j*

a small animal that lives in a shell → *sn*

to not pass a test → *f*

7 Write '**–ail**' or '**–oil**' in the spaces to make words from the Word List.
Write the complete words in your book.

sn _ _ _ fr _ _ _ br _ _ _ qu _ _ _ f _ _ _ p _ _ _

RHYME time › Copy this rhyme into your book and then ...

1. Circle all the '**–ail**' words.
2. Draw a square around the '**–oil**' words.

Yo, ho, ho! Who are we?
We are sailors
On the boiling sea.
And we sing as we sail

In the sun, rain or hail,
Yo, ho, ho! Sailors free,
Singing as we sail
On the boiling sea.

WORD KNOWLEDGE > Compound words

RULE

Compound words are two words that join to make one larger word, for example: *rail* + *way* = *railway*.

1 Join these words together to make a compound word.
Write the complete words in your book.

in + to = ______ bed + room = ______ sail + board = ______

bull + frog = ______ her + self = ______ some + how = ______

2 Copy these tables into your book. Draw lines to connect words that make compound words.
Write the complete words in your book.

bath	port
break	fast
day	room
cow	boy
bed	time
him	bell
car	self
door	light

COMMON WORDS >

Choose words from the Spelling List to fill the gaps.
Write the complete sentences in your book.

1. _ _ _ town is near the coast.
2. The football player could _ _ _ _ the ball very far.
3. We saw the _ _ _ _ _ slide across the grass.
4. I don't know _ _ _ to fix the car.
5. We had _ _ _ people staying at our house.

Weekly Spelling List to be tested at the end of the week

Spelling LIST

our
kick
jumped
how
six
snail
oil
sail
soil
spoil

Writing activity

- Make a list of all the things that you can find in, on or near the sea.
Then write about a time when you went to the sea to fish, swim or play.

FOCUS › '–t' words

Word LIST

beet
feet
meet
fleet
greet
sheet
sleet
street
sweet
tweet
boot
hoot
loot
moot
root
toot
scoot
shoot

1 Choose the correct word. Write the complete sentences in your book.

a. The teacher wrote the answer on a (sleet / sheet) of paper.

b. The police van drove down the (sweet / street) very slowly.

c. We put our bags in the (loot / boot) of our car.

d. The robbers buried the (toot / loot) from the robbery under a tree.

e. The (root / shoot) system of the oak tree is very large.

f. We will (beet / greet) our relatives with flowers.

2 Find words for the pictures in the Word List.
Write the words in sentences in your book.

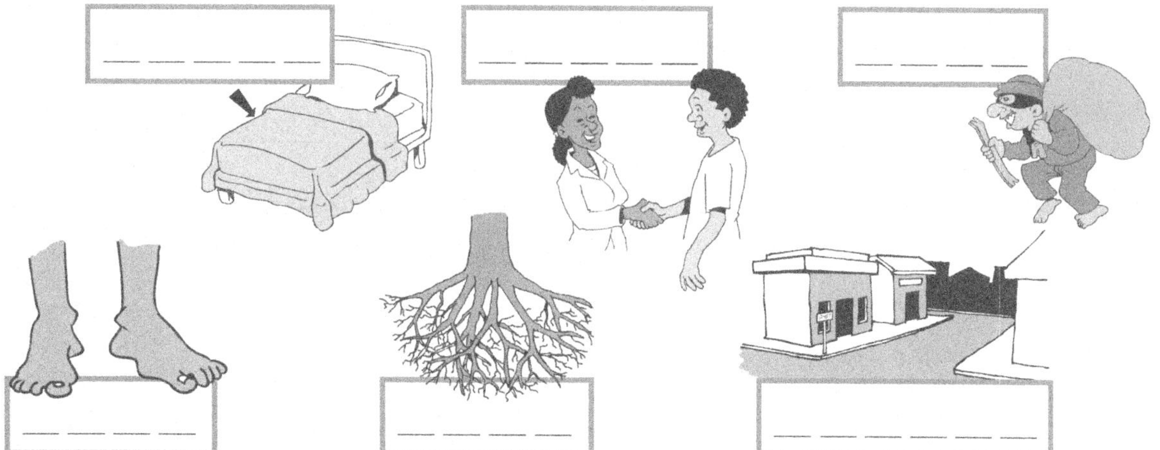

3 Choose words from the Spelling List to fill the gaps.
Write the complete sentences in your book.

a. Aunty has blisters on her _ _ _ _.

b. We put all our shopping in the car _ _ _ _.

c. We will _ _ _ _ _ our friends on Saturday.

d. The pineapple was very _ _ _ _ _ to eat.

4 Copy these word grids into your book.
Change one letter in each grid to make a new word that matches the picture.

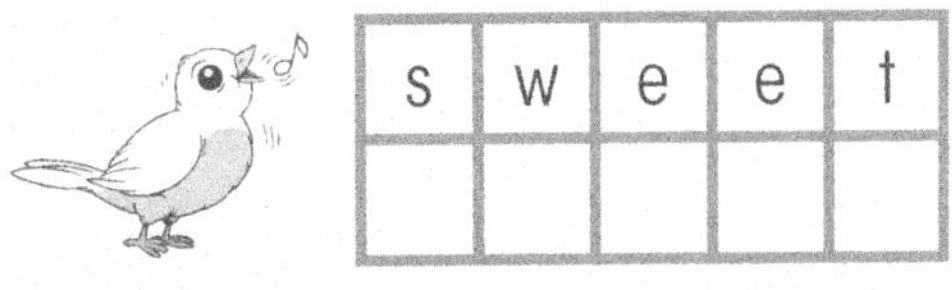

s	w	e	e	t

b	o	o	t

f	e	e	t

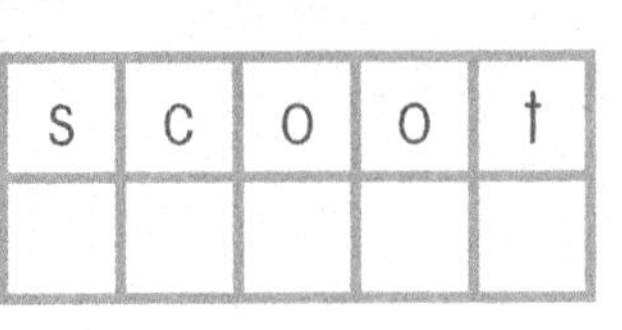

s	c	o	o	t

m	o	o	t

5 Write as many words as you can with the magic word machine, for example:
sh + ee + t = sheet.

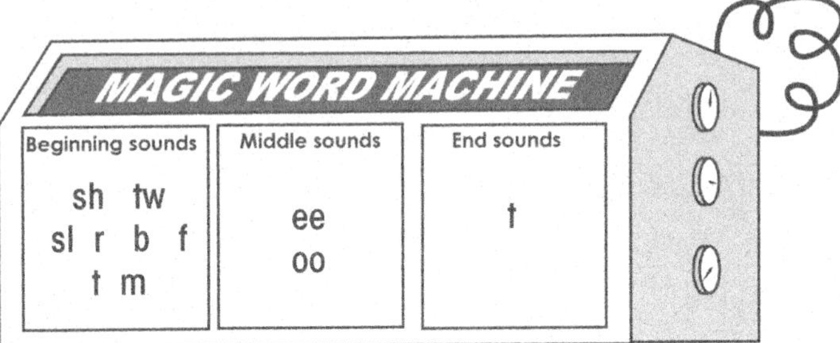

6 Find words from the Word List that have a similar meaning to these words.
Write the words in sentences in your book. The first one has been done for you.

dirt → *soot* *The soot from the drum oven was very black and hot.*

a bird call → *tw* ______

stolen money → *l* ______

on the end of your legs → *f* ______

a piece of paper → *sh* ______

7 Write '**–oot**' or '**–eet**' in the spaces to make words from the Word List.
Write the words in your book.

sh _ _ _   sh _ _ _   sc _ _ _   str _ _ _

RHYME time › Copy this rhyme into your book and then ...

Circle all the '**–eet**' words.

Tweet, tweet!
Girl on street
Waits to meet
Someone sweet.

Tweet, tweet!
Bird on street
Waits to greet
Someone sweet.

Girl . . . street,
Bird . . . greet,
Both . . . meet,
That's . . . sweet!

WORD KNOWLEDGE > Adjectives and nouns

✱ RULE

Remember that **nouns** are **naming** words and **adjectives** are **describing** words.
Adjectives tell us more about nouns, for example: a *big* tree, a *green* roof, a *hot* drink.

Choose the correct words from the Adjective Box to fill the gaps.
Write the complete sentences in your book.

Adjective BOX

loud big sweet thick old ripe

1. The giant had _ _ _ feet.
2. It was a very _ _ _ _ _ drink.
3. The car made a _ _ _ _ toot.
4. The _ _ _ boot had holes in it.
5. The tree had a _ _ _ _ _ root.
6. The pawpaw was very _ _ _ _ .

COMMON WORDS >

Choose words from the Spelling List to fill the gaps.
Write the complete sentences in your book.

1. "_ _ _ _ _ are you going?" asked the teacher.
2. The villagers had to walk very far to collect _ _ _ _ _ from the river.
3. I have _ _ _ cockatoos in a cage at home.
4. "Where are _ _ _ _ shoes?" asked Mum.
5. I have _ _ _ _ _ brothers and sisters in my family.
6. We were told that we had to be home by _ _ _ _ _ o'clock.

Spelling LIST

where
water
two
your
seven
eight
scoot
feet
meet
sweet

Writing activity

- Write about an animal you really like.
  Describe the animal and say why you like it.
  When you have finished, underline all the adjectives you have used in your sentences.

Revision

FOCUS > '–rk' '–rt' '–il' '–t' words

1 Copy this table into your book.
Write words from the Word List into the correct box.

–ark	–ork

2 Copy this table into your book.
Write words from the Word List into the correct box.

–art	–irt	–ort	–urt

3 Write these words in sentences in your book.

skirt sport fork spark dark fork bark flirt

4 Use words from the Word List to fill the gaps.
Write the complete sentences in your book.

a. The pigs began to ______ and grunt when it was time to eat.

b. The ______ from the fire landed on the grass.

c. The teacher tripped over and ______ his leg.

d. I listened to the dog ______ all night.

e. You must not go outside after it is ______.

5 Write each of these pairs of words in a sentence in your book.

dark / park fork / pork

Word LIST

sport
bark
cart
cork
dirt
dark
hark
fork
pork
part
tart
blurt
skirt
hurt
stark
splurt
sport
squirt
start
curt
snort
short
flirt
chart
spark
shark
smart
sort
port

Word LIST

scoot
tweet
spoil
trail
bail
fail
boil
coil
beet
feet
boot
toot
shoot
sweet
broil
snail
jail
foil
meet
fleet
loot
root
sleet
toil
soil
sail
tail
mail
oil
greet
sheet
hoot
quail

6 Copy this table into your book.
Write words from the Word List into the correct boxes.

–ail	–oil

7 Copy this table into your book.
Write words from the Word List into the correct boxes.

–oot	–eet

8 Write these words in sentences of your own in your book.

sheet foil toot sail trail soil spoil

9 Use words from the Word List to fill the gaps.
Write the complete sentences in your book.

a. The hunters followed the cassowary _ _ _ _ _ in the bush.
b. The _ _ _ _ _ slid across the path.
c. It is good to wash your _ _ _ _ before you go to bed.
d. The _ _ _ from the car dripped onto the road.
e. I will _ _ _ _ _ my friend at the bus stop.
f. The yacht let out its _ _ _ _ when the wind began to blow.

10 Write each of these pairs of words in a sentence in your book.

meet / greet spoil / soil

Get off the lizard!

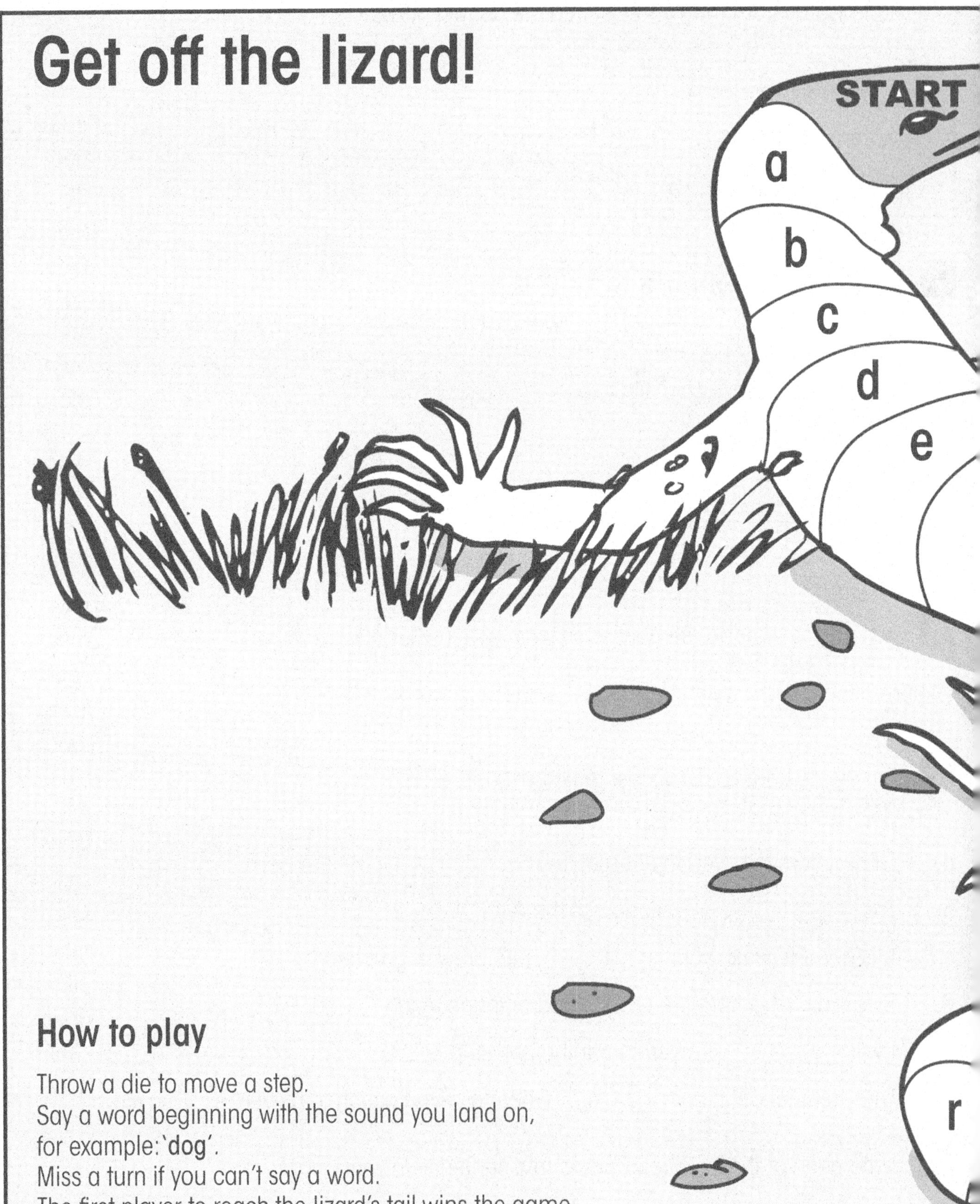

How to play

Throw a die to move a step.
Say a word beginning with the sound you land on, for example: '**dog**'.
Miss a turn if you can't say a word.
The first player to reach the lizard's tail wins the game.

h
i
j
k
l
m
n
o
p
t
u
v
w
x
y
z
FINISH

Get off the python!

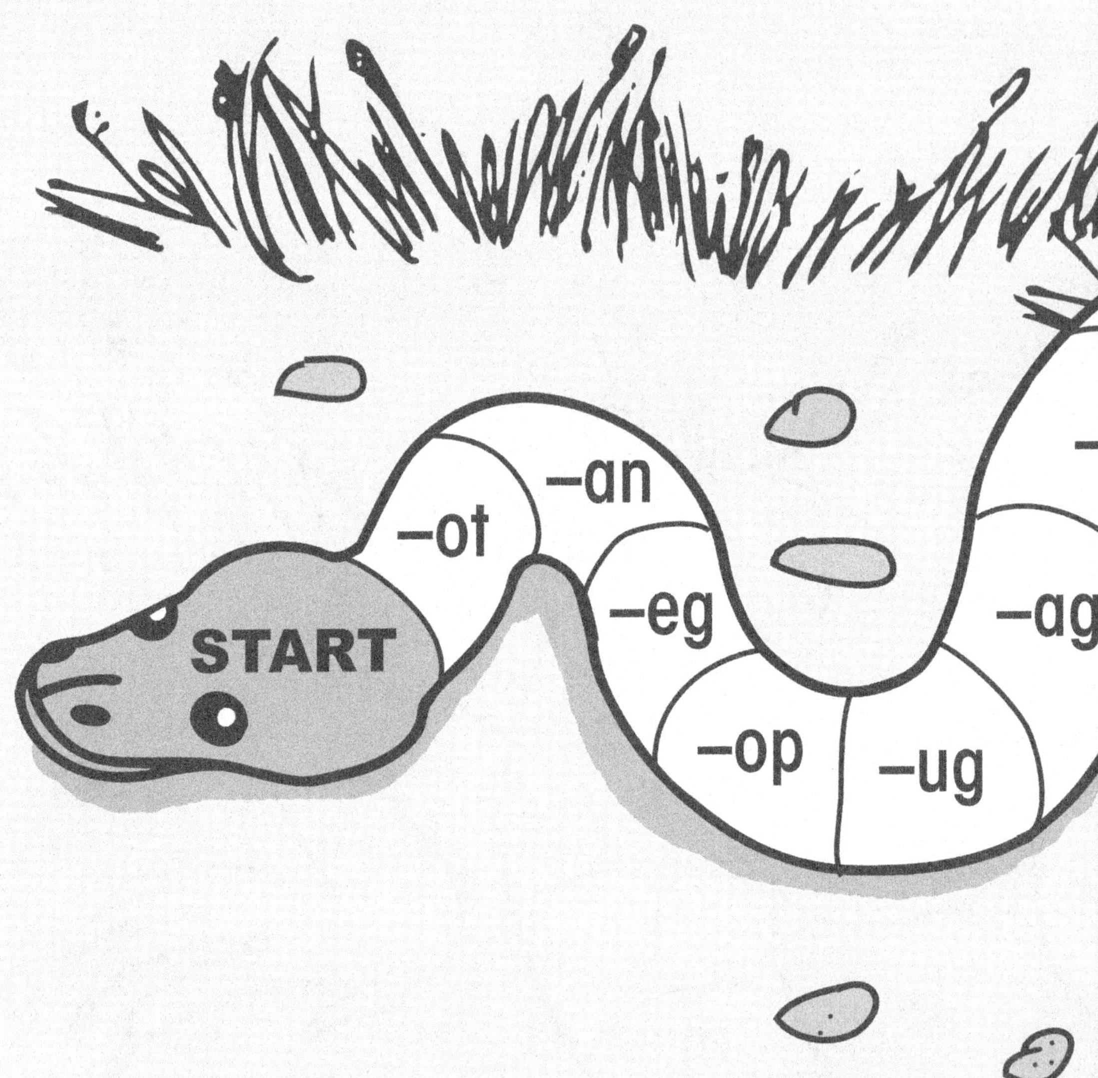

How to play

Throw a die to move a step.
Add a beginning sound to the word ending you land on to make a word,
for example: c + at = **cat**.
Miss a turn if you can't make a word.
The first player to reach the lizard's tail wins the game.

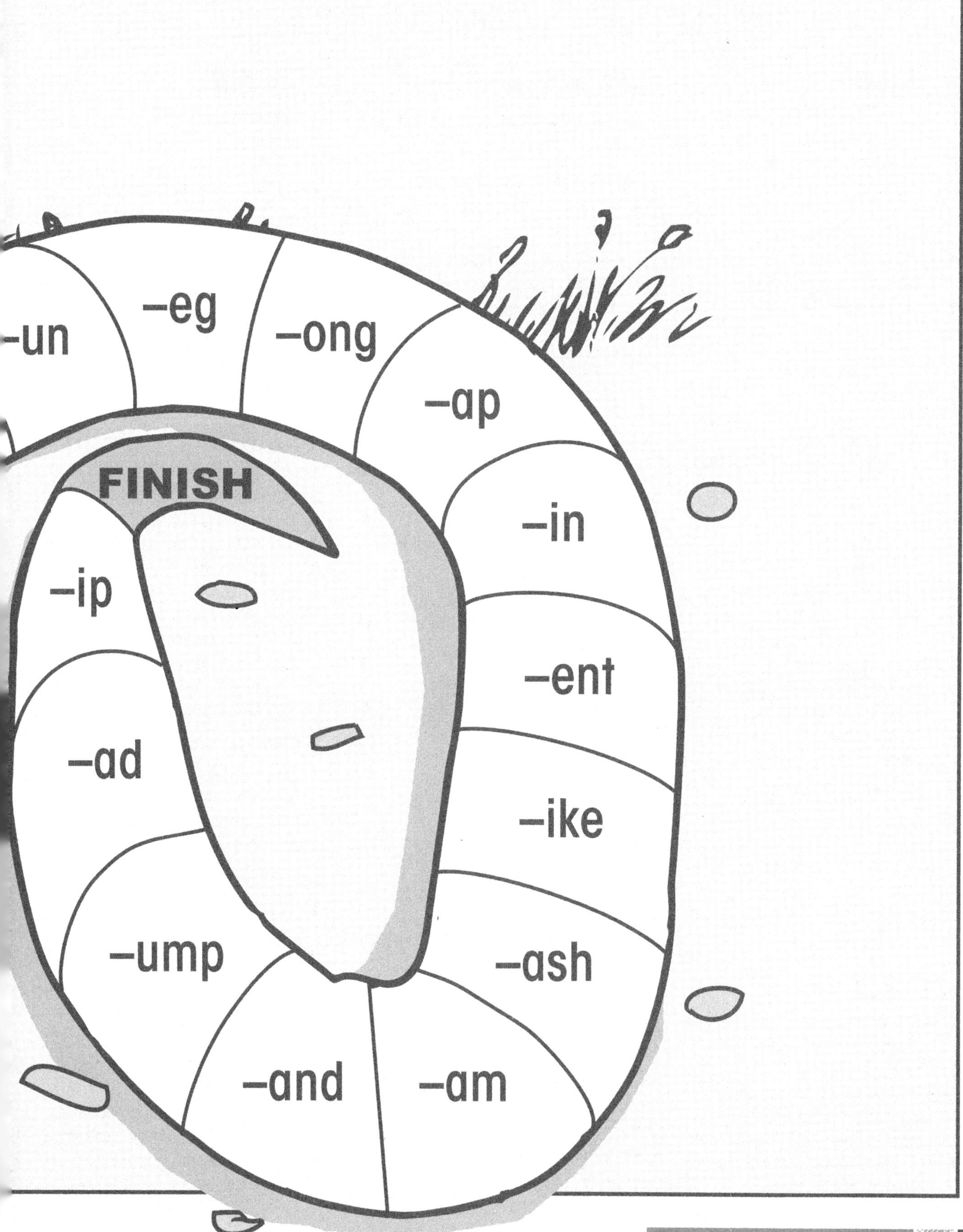

-un
-eg
-ong
-ap
FINISH
-in
-ip
-ent
-ad
-ike
-ump
-ash
-and
-am

Answers

Unit 1

2 ant/arrow, banana/boy, coconut, drum/dog, egg/elbow, fire/fish, girl/garden, hat/hammer, ink, jar/jug
3 baby, hand, egg, ant, dress, apple, fish, igloo, hair, exit, jet, horse, jar, candle, cave, bike, gate, hat, grass, canoe
4 Possible answers: egg, dress, fish, gate, baby, candle, hair, igloo, jar
5 dam, jam, ham, Sam, ram
6 cap, gap, lap, map, sap, tap

WORD KNOWLEDGE ›

1 A, B, C, D, E, F, G, H, I, J, K, L, N, Q, R, S, T, U, V, W, X, Y, Z.
M, O, P are missing.
2 a, b, c, d, e, f, g, h, i, j, k, l, m, o, p, q, r, t, v, w, x, y, z.
n, s, u are missing.

Unit 2

2 king/key, log/leg/ladder, moon/mango, nose/nest, orange/octopus, pan/pumpkin, queen/quack, rabbit/rose
3 on, kennel, peas, map, queen, lizard, rat, off, leg, roof, kitten, man, potato, nut, question, needle
4 Possible answers: potato, kennel, queen, nut, man, on, lizard, rat

WORD KNOWLEDGE ›

1 a b c d e f g h i j k l m n o p q r s t u v w x y z
2 A B C D E F G H I J K L M N O P Q R S T U V W X Y Z
3 w, c, n, g, h, l, x, u, z, k, d, a, u, q, x, o; O, E, F, S, W, P, T, M, Q, L

Unit 3

2 spider/sun/six, table, umbrella/under, volcano, watch/window, xylophone, yacht/yawn, zip
3 tart, shell, van, tiger, yolk, whale, zigzag, tent, window, snake, lizard, zip, yoyo, umpire, spider, x-ray
4 Possible answers: yoyo, tart, window, x-ray, van, umpire, zigzag

Unit 4 REVISION

FOCUS › Revise letter names and sounds
2 b c g h j o r t v y

FOCUS › Lower case letter order
1 a, b, c, d, e, f, g, h, i, j, k, l, m, n, o, p, q, r, s, t, u, v, w, x, y, z.

FOCUS › Upper case letter order
1 Goroka, July, Mr Potek, Port Moresby, Tuesday; girl, hat, jug, teacher, window

Unit 5

1 pan, man, fan, van can
2 cat, hat, mat, rat
3 cap, tap, map, zap
4 jam, ham, yam, dam; dad, pad, lad, sad; rag, wag, sag, bag
5 dam, jam, ham, Sam, ram
6 cap, gap, lap, map, rap, sap, tap, yap, zap, etc.

WORD KNOWLEDGE ›

1 a, b, c, d, e, f, g, h, i, j, k, l, m, n, o, p, q, r, t, v, x, y
2 s, u, w, z

COMMON WORDS ›

1 dad; **2** you; **3** that; **4** and

Unit 6

1 wed, sped, fed, bed
2 men, hen, pen, ten
3 wet, pet, vet, net
4 hen, ten, men, pen; red, wed, fed, led; net, pet, bet, wet
5 wet, pet, bet, beg, leg, peg, wed, bed, led, web, pen, ten, den
6 wet, pet, bet; beg, leg, peg; wed, bed, led; web; pen, ten, den

WORD KNOWLEDGE ›

1 a, b, c, d, e, f, g, h, i, j, k, l, m, n, o, p, q, r, t, v, x, y
2 s, u, w, z

COMMON WORDS ›

1 hen; **2** bell; **3** four; **4** are; **5** fish

Unit 7

1 slip, ship, sip, zip, drib
2 pin, bin, fin, grin
3 lid, hid, kid, slid
4 lid, rid, kid, did; big, pig, jig, rig; in, skin, tin, win
5 pig, fig, twig, wig, big, rig

WORD KNOWLEDGE ›

ant, axe; egg, eskimo; insect, imp; ostrich, orange; under, unhappy

COMMON WORDS ›

1 but; **2** have; **3** win; **4** with; **5** be

Unit 8

1 cot, pot, hot, dot
2 top, chop, hop, mop
3 dog, frog, log, jog
4 top, pop, hop, mop; mob, sob, job, rob; not, rot, cot, hot
5 Many answers, for example: cop, cob, cot, cod, cog, etc.
6 Many answers, for example: cop, hop, mop; job, lob, mob; not, lot, got; nod, pod, rod; hog, bog, jog, etc.

WORD KNOWLEDGE ›

1 ant, arrow; elephant, egg, end; ice cream, ink, igloo; octopus, orange, off; umbrella, umpire, under
1 5 vowels, 21 consonants

COMMON WORDS ›

1 stop; **2** up; **3** on; **4** shop; **5** dog

Unit 9

1 rug, hug, mug, bug, jug
2 sun, run, bun, spun
3 mum, drum, plum, sum
4 gum, plum, swum; rug, tug, plug; sun, run, bun, fun
5 bug, tug, hug, mud, dud, bud, shun, stun, fun, hum, glum, plum
6 bug, tug, hug; mud, dud, bud; shun, stun, fun; hum, glum, plum

WORD KNOWLEDGE ›

1 Sunday, sunbake, suntan, sunshine, sunlight, sunburn
2 playschool, playroom, playground, playmate

COMMON WORDS ›

1 sum; **2** she; **3** when; **4** at; **5** bug, jug

Unit 10 REVISION

1 pan, jab, bat, man, rat;
leg, pen, net;
pit, did; mop, pot;
jug, sun, bug, hut
2 **a** hot; **b** jug; **c** man; **d** leg; **e** pen

Unit 11

1 hand, land, band;
mend, bend, send, lend, blend;
bond, pond, blond
2 pond, hand, send
3 send, bend, tend, mend;
land, sand, band, hand
4 **a** hand; **b** pond; **c** wind; **d** blond;
e send; **f** band; **g** bend
5 **a** sand; **b** mend; **c** pond; **d** stand;
e hand

COMMON WORDS ›

1 out; **2** pond; **3** were; **4** like; **5** all

Unit 12

1 brick, pocket, back, clock, peck, lick, truck, black, quick, neck, tick, rock, luck, tack
2 sick, chick, sock, lick, neck, rock
3 lick, brick, kick, quick, trick, slick;
clock, tock, flock, block, sock, knock
4 pack, stack, sack; peck, neck;
pick, sick, tick, stick; clock, sock;
suck, struck, pluck
5 **a** duck; **b** suck; **c** tick; **d** stick; **e** peck;
f pack; **g** sack
6 **a** stuck; **b** pack; **c** neck; **d** clock; **e** sock

WORD KNOWLEDGE ›

People – Jack, Jock, Mick
Places – Papua New Guinea, Australia, Lae
Animals – duck, chick
Things – rock, sock, clock, truck, neck, frock, stick

COMMON WORDS ›

1 be; **2** see; **3** eat; **4** just; **5** not

Unit 13

1 sank, pink, drink, sink, wink, tank, bunk, sunk, junk, drank, trunk, stunk
2 drink, sink, ink, clink, blink
3 Many answers, for example:
blank, crank, drank, shrank, thank, etc.
4 thank, bank, sank, spank, drank;
shrink, clink, pink, link, wink, blink;
hunk, chunk, bunk, junk
5 Many answers, for example:
The boy is having a drink with his feet in the sink.
6 **a** sank; **b** junk; **c** drank; **d** pink; **e** bank
7 **a** thank; **b** bunk; **c** shrink; **d** spank

WORD KNOWLEDGE ›

1 **a** me; **b** them; **c** him; **d** her
2 **a** We; **b** he; **c** them; **d** she

COMMON WORDS ›

1 did; **2** very; **3** then; **4** so

Unit 14

1 string, gang, sing, strong, king, long, bang, song, wing, gong, hung
2 wing, sting, sing, king, sling, spring
3 hung, lung, sung, slung, stung, swung
4 sing, ring, king, sling;
long, song, strong, gong
5 rang, slang, bang, clang, gang;
thing, bring, wing, swing, sling;
strong, wrong, long, dong;
lung, sung, stung, swung
6 **a** long; **b** bang; **c** strong; **d** wing;
e stung; **f** bring
7 **a** sing; **b** wrong; **c** sling; **d** gang;
e clang

WORD KNOWLEDGE ›

1 Various for each child
2 Thursday, Sunday;
March, June, August, November

COMMON WORDS ›

1 go; **2** from; **3** no; **4** came; **5** do

Unit 15 REVISION

1 bland, and, sand, land, stand, brand;
lend, send, bend;
pond, fond
2 back, tack, sack, black;
neck, peck, wreck, speck;
quick, stick, sick, lick; rock, clock;
luck, truck, cluck
3 **a** pond; **b** peck; **c** quick; **d** truck;
e send; **f** lack
5 thank, spank, shrank, plank, tank, blank; drink, clink, stink, blink, kink;
bunk, junk, trunk, hunk, stunk, chunk, slunk
6 gang, rang, sang, clang, bang;
swing, thing, string; bong, long;
hung, lung, sung, slung
7 **a** trunk; **b** sang; **c** drink; **d** thank;
e gang; **f** bang
8 Many answers

Unit 16

1 pest, test, west, nest, vest;
crust, just, rust, must, bust, dust;
lost and list don't belong
2 vest, crust, fist, chest
3 frost, lost, cost; twist, list, fist
5 **a** nest; **b** lost; **c** vest; **d** pest; **e** crust;
f gust, dust
6 **a** rest; **b** pest; **c** rust; **d** list; **e** mist
7 test, gust, crust, wrist

WORD KNOWLEDGE ›

1 tall tree, exotic flower, winding road, ripe pawpaw, green banana, hard coconut, smelly fish, angry cat, fat pig, large village

COMMON WORDS ›

1 family; **2** dad; **3** mum; **4** on; **5** came

Unit 17

1 dump, lump, stump, jump, pump, bump;
camp, ramp, clamp, stamp;
limp and romp do not belong
2 stump, pump, stamp, chimp
3 romp, chomp, stomp;
thump, slump, grump
4 **a** camp; **b** hump; **c** chimp; **d** stump;
e damp; **f** stamp
5 **a** limp; **b** camp; **c** jump; **d** plump;
e chomp
6 jump, chimp, dump

WORD KNOWLEDGE ›

1 village, fishing, rocky, rocky, rough, spotted, spotted, green, village, great

COMMON WORDS ›

1 from; **2** had; **3** have; **4** has; **5** went

Unit 18

1 cash, bash, mash, smash;
dish, fish, wish, swish;
rush and crush don't belong
2 dish, cash, brush, smash
3 smash, flash, crash; rush, flush, crush
5 **a** fish; **b** dash; **c** sash; **d** rush;
e cash; **f** wish
6 **a** fish; **b** rush; **c** brush; **d** gash; **e** lash
7 blush, cash, crash

WORD KNOWLEDGE ›

1 trees, flowers, roads, pawpaws, bananas, cats, pigs, villages, books, teachers

COMMON WORDS ›

1 as; **2** ask; **3** big; **4** by; **5** of

Unit 19

1 mint, print, sprint, hint; bent, sent, cent, spent; pant and hunt do not belong
2 tent, dent, ant, sprint
3 blunt, stunt, grunt; grant, rant, chant
5 **a** sent; **b** splint; **c** grunt; **d** hunt;
e ant; **f** blunt
6 **a** lent; **b** spent; **c** mint; **d** slant; **e** chant
7 bent, dent, rent

WORD KNOWLEDGE ›

1 car, truck, pig, driver, brake, pig, man, woman, pig, village, car, truck
2 **a** three; **b** twelve; **c** three; **d** six

COMMON WORDS ›

1 She; **2** him; **3** her; **4** fish; **5** He

Unit 20 REVISION

1 test, chest, west, rest, vest;
fist, twist, list, mist; lost, cost;
dust, just, trust, gust, bust, must
2 champ, stamp, cramp; limp;
romp, chomp; bump, rump, jump, thump, stump, dump
3 **a** list; **b** test; **c** stamp; **d** dust; **e** lost
5 flash, smash, crash, ash, cash, sash, dash, trash; fish, swish, dish;
rush, blush, crush, hush, slush
6 pant, grant, chant, slant;
cent, rent, bent, dent, lent, sent;
hint, tint, dint, glint, print;
grunt, stunt, runt, hunt, blunt
7 **a** smash; **b** hunt; **c** grunt; **d** dish;
e cash; **f** fish; **g** spent; **h** dent

Unit 21

1 doll, troll, toll, roll;
bell, fell, smell, well, yell;
bill, chill, pill, hill
2 doll, bill, well, hill, bell, troll
3 smell, spell, tell; chill, pill, dill
4 **a** shell; **b** fell; **c** well; **d** Will; **e** doll
5 well, spell, pill, chill, bell, ill
6 Answers can vary.
Possible answers: doll, roll, troll;
bell, dell, fell; bill, dill, fill;
fell, well, yell
7 Possible answers: doll, roll, stroll, toll, fill, will, hill, chill, bell, dell, spell

WORD KNOWLEDGE ›

1 foxes, tomatoes, watches, matches, wishes, echoes, mangoes, classes, potatoes
2 teachers, brushes, desks, glasses, dishes, towns, villages, cakes, classes, tables, gardens, helpers, taxes, boxes, flowers, heroes, volcanoes
3 fox, piano, wish, school, match

COMMON WORDS ›

1 food; **2** smell; **3** you; **4** Will; **5** Yes

Unit 22

1 fern, stern; barn, yarn, darn;
corn, worn, thorn, scorn, horn, sworn;
burn, turn
2 fern, barn, corn, torn, burn, shorn
3 scorn, torn, sworn, horn, thorn,
worn, born, corn;
burn, churn, turn, spurn
4 **a** born; **b** torn; **c** burn; **d** turn;
e stern; **f** worn
5 circle 'bake' and 'time'
6 Answers can vary.
Possible answers:
corn, born, horn, morn, torn;
stern; yarn; burn, spurn
7 Possible answers:
barn, fern, turn, born, torn, yarn, morn, tern, thorn, stern, sworn

WORD KNOWLEDGE ›

1 children; **2** geese; **3** mice; **4** women;
5 feet; **6** men; **7** people

COMMON WORDS ›

1 into; **2** here; **3** going; **4** little; **5** house

Unit 23

1 match, catch, latch, scratch,
patch, hatch;
ditch, itch, stitch, switch, witch;
fetch, sketch, wretch; clutch, hutch
2 witch, itch, patch, catch, hatch, match
3 hatch, thatch, match, catch, scratch,
patch; witch, pitch, stitch, hitch,
switch, ditch
4 **a** catch; **b** patch; **c** witch; **d** hutch
5 circle 'jump', 'doll', 'learn', 'bike'
6 Answers can vary. Possible answers:
batch, catch, hatch; sketch, wretch;
pitch, hitch, switch; crutch
7 Possible answers: batch, hitch, botch, clutch, pitch, patch, latch, catch, switch, hutch

WORD KNOWLEDGE ›

2 **a** cut; **b** walk; **c** jump; **d** swim; **e** climb

COMMON WORDS ›

1 fetch; **2** what; **3** morning; **4** night;
5 make

Unit 24

1 gale, male, whale, scale, sale,
stale, bale; file, smile, tile, while;
hole, mole, pole, role, stole, whole;
mule, rule
2 mule, smile, pole, whale, sale, hole
3 **a** hole; **b** pole; **c** whale; **d** rule; **e** stale
4 Many answers, for example:
gale, rule, smile, whole
5 circle 'help', 'sell', 'show', 'walk', 'her'
6 sale, rule, pile
7 Possible answers: sale, hole, file, rule, role, mile, gale, scale, mule, while, hole

WORD KNOWLEDGE ›

1 run, skip, walk, stretch
2 **a** run; **b** catch; **c** walk; **d** scratch;
e stretch

COMMON WORDS ›

1 off; **2** played; **3** looked; **4** in; **5** one

Unit 25 REVISION

1 toll, stroll, roll;
smell, spell, yell, dell, well; chill, bill, hill
2 darn, yarn, barn; stern;
torn, horn, worn, morn, shorn;
spurn, turn, churn, burn
4 **a** worn; **b** burn; **c** hill; **d** turn; **e** shorn

6 catch, scratch, match, hatch, latch, thatch, batch, patch; etch; wretch; itch, switch, witch, pitch
7 pale, whale, sale, gale, stale; while, tile, file, smile; pole, stole, hole, role, mole; mule, capsule, rule
9 **a** hatch; **b** gale; **c** pale; **d** catch; **e** patch; **f** pole

Unit 26

1 came, same, flame, shame, game, name, tame; lime, crime, chime, grime, mime, slime; home, dome
3 frame, game, lime, flame
4 dome, gnome, chrome; grime, chime, mime
5 **a** name; **b** slime; **c** frame; **d** name, same, name; **e** home
6 home, frame, mime, flame, gnome, tame
7 Answers can vary. Possible answers: grime, time, slime; dame, fame, lame; home, gnome
8 shame, grime, blame, slime

WORD KNOWLEDGE ›

1 **a** shouted; **b** jumped; **c** played; **d** fished

COMMON WORDS ›

1 saw; 2 under; 3 them; 4 tree; 5 because

Unit 27

1 bake, wake, brake, snake, cake, fake; bike, hike, like, spike; woke, smoke
3 cake, snake, bike, rake
4 **a** hike; **b** broke; **c** drive; **d** make, cake; **e** like
5 broke, stroke, joke; drake, brake, flake
6 drake, bike, joke, wake, cake, snake
7 Answers can vary. Possible answers: joke, poke, smoke; hike, like, bike; cake, make, snake
8 hike, snake, smoke, spike or spoke, flake

WORD KNOWLEDGE ›

1 **a** walk/walked; **b** see/saw; **c** ride/rode; **d** tell/told; **e** cry/cried

COMMON WORDS ›

1 after; 2 said; 3 name; 4 Where; 5 very

Unit 28

1 space, lace, race, place, grace, trace; price, twice, nice, rice
3 face, dice, mice, slice
5 **a** slice; **b** mice; **c** dice; **d** lice; **e** space
6 Possible answers: race, grace; lace, place; pace, space
7 twice, rice, spice, space, face, mice
8 Answers can vary. Possible answers: face, pace; price, twice; grace, place; rice, nice
9 slice, nice, dice, twice, grace

WORD KNOWLEDGE ›

1 **a** working; **b** building; **c** walking; **d** Singing; **e** jumping

COMMON WORDS ›

1 brother; 2 sister; 3 down; 4 This; 5 give

Unit 29

1 mine, shine, pine, nine; tone, phone, bone; pane, lane, plane
3 spine, phone, plane, crane
4 **a** mane; **b** stone; **c** fine; **d** nine; **e** crane
6 spine, nine, stone, swine, plane
7 Answers can vary. Possible answers: line, pine, vine; crane, vane, sane; stone, phone, bone; shine, wine, twine; lane, sane, plane; clone, tone, cone
8 plane, spine, stone, whine, shine or shone

WORD KNOWLEDGE ›

1 tightly, carefully, neatly, firmly, slowly, nicely
2 **a** loudly; **b** quietly; **c** quickly; **d** slowly; **e** noisily

COMMON WORDS ›

1 was; 2 quickly; 3 quietly; 4 people; 5 play

Unit 30 REVISION

1 came, fame, lame, name, tame, dame, shame; time, chime, lime, mime, grime, slime; home, gnome, dome
2 bake, take, cake, make, brake; bike, hike, like, spike; joke, stroke, spoke, smoke, broke
4 **a** spoke; **b** came; **c** home; **d** smoke; **e** cake
6 grace, race, space, pace, place, trace, lace; ice, lice, nice, rice, mice, dice, slice
7 plane, lane, cane, mane, sane; line, fine, mine, nine, shine, spine; clone, phone, tone, lone, cone, zone, bone
9 **a** plane; **b** mice; **c** race; **d** nine; **e** phone; **f** line

Unit 31

1 **a** bride; **b** rode; **c** code; **d** rude; **e** glide; **f** tide
2 code, bride, blade, slide, shade, hide
3 blade, grade; bride, glide
4 Many answers, for example: stride, grade
5 blade, shade, nude, wide
6 **a** ride; **b** rode; **c** rude; **d** bide; **e** bride; **f** side; **g** bade **h** ode
7 **a** Hide the cash under the tree.
b Where are you hiding?
c Escape now!
d You are being followed.

WORD KNOWLEDGE ›

1 **b** I'm; **c** don't **d** he's; **e** she's; **f** can't; **g** didn't

COMMON WORDS ›

1 don't; 2 has 3 It's; 4 I'm; 5 home

Unit 32

1 **a** white; **b** crate; **c** bite; **d** plate; **e** ate; **f** write
2 plate, gate, bite, kite
3 hate, fate, late
4 Many answers, for example: late, write, white
5 white, hate, crate, late
6 **a** gate; **b** state; **c** kite; **d** skite; **e** late; **f** grade
7 **a** We will meet you at the gate.
b What is the secret code?
c Get here quickly!
d It is time to go.

WORD KNOWLEDGE ›

1 he's – he is; let's – let us; it's – it is; she's – she is; we're – we are; can't – can not; I'm – I am
2 **a** she's; **b** I'm; **c** isn't; **d** we're; **e** didn't; **f** let's

Answers

COMMON WORDS ›

1 away; **2** gate; **3** old; **4** write; **5** car

Unit 33

1 **a** boy; **b** stay; **c** hay; **d** sway; **e** joy; **f** tray
2 pay, play, toy, boy
3 clay, pray, way
5 Many answers, for example: sway, tray, toy
6 boy, day, tray, pray
7 Possible answers: play, tray, stray, spray

WORD KNOWLEDGE ›

1 hot, cold; new, old; tall, short; boy, girl; yes, no
2 soft, short, low, old, shut, smooth

COMMON WORDS ›

1 every; **2** first; **3** get; **4** got; **5** very

Unit 34

1 **a** meat; **b** neat; **c** goat; **d** throat; **e** heat; **f** moat
2 meat, goat, coat, seat, heat
3 heat, meat, seat; boat, gloat, coat
4 Many answers, for example: bleat, throat, bloat
5 neat, bleat, boat, seat
6 feat, heat, coat, cheat, throat, float, seat, goat, treat

WORD KNOWLEDGE ›

1 **a** First, Then; **b** Next, After that; **c** Finally
2 **a** First; **b** Next;**c** Then; **d** Finally

COMMON WORDS ›

1 over; **2** Put; **3** fix; **4** some; **5** one

Unit 35 REVISION

1 bride, hide, ride, slide, inside; fade, made, grade, blade, shade; code, strode, rode
2 ate, grate, plate, state, date, rate; bite, kite, white, quite, mite, site
4 **a** write; **b** blade; **c** bite; **d** shade; **e** rode
6 stray, sway, play, ray, lay, may, tray, say, pray, way, bay, spray; boy, coy, joy, toy, soy, ploy
8 beat, heat, bleat, cheat, pleat, neat; boat, goat, float, coat, bloat, throat, oat
9 **a** boat; **b** throat; **c** play; **d** stray; **e** float

Unit 36

1 **a** bark; **b** shark; **c** dark; **d** mark; **e** cork; **f** stork
2 fork, spark, pork, shark
3 bark, dark, lark; cork, fork, stork
4 Many answers, for example: fork, mark, spark
5 fork, shark, pork, bark
6 **a** pork; **b** shark; **c** cork; **d** spark; **e** fork; **f** hark
7 **a** Mark the spot with an x.
b Come quickly!
c Need help now!
d When will we meet?

WORD KNOWLEDGE ›

1 unwise, unsafe, unfriendly, unfit, unsure, unkind, unhappy, unfair

COMMON WORDS ›

1 door; **2** two, two; **3** three, two; **4** four; **5** five

Unit 37

1 **a** skirt; **b** sport; **c** tart; **d** port; **e** short; **f** snort
2 dart, port, cart, chart, fort, shirt
3 shirt, short; sport, spurt; chart; blurt
4 shirt, start, short, port
5 Many answers, for example: squirt, chart, flirt
6 port, smart, snort, cart
7 short or shirt, squirt, flirt, sport or spurt, tart, dart or dirt, snort, skirt

WORD KNOWLEDGE ›

1 shortest, quicker, hardest, taller, tallest

COMMON WORDS ›

1 their; **2** fun; **3** school; **4** room; **5** too

Unit 38

1 **a** tail; **b** sail; **c** oil; **d** soil; **e** boil; **f** frail
2 trail, mail, boil, snail, coil, quail
3 **a** snail, trail; **b** nail; **c** frail; **d** tail
4 sail, tail, mail, boil
5 Many answers, for example: spoil, bail, toil
6 frail, jail, snail, fail
7 snail, frail, broil, quail, fail/foil, pail

WORD KNOWLEDGE ›

1 into, bedroom, sailboard, bullfrog, herself, somehow
2 bathtime, breakfast, daylight, cowboy, himself, carport, doorbell

COMMON WORDS ›

1 Our; **2** kick; **3** snail; **4** how; **5** six

Unit 39

1 **a** sheet; **b** street; **c** boot; **d** loot; **e** root; **f** greet
2 sheet, greet, loot, feet, root, street
3 **a** feet; **b** boot; **c** meet; **d** sweet
4 tweet, shoot, root, loot, meet
5 Many answers, for example: sheet, feet, toot
6 tweet, loot, feet, sheet
7 shoot, sheet, scoot, street

WORD KNOWLEDGE ›

1 big; **2** sweet; **3** loud; **4** old; **5** thick; **6** ripe

COMMON WORDS ›

1 Where; **2** water; **3** two; **4** your; **5** seven/eight; **6** seven/eight

Unit 40 REVISION

1 bark, dark, hark, stark, spark, shark; cork, fork, pork
2 cart, part, tart, start, chart, smart; dirt, flirt, skirt, squirt; sport, snort, short, sort, port; blurt, hurt, splurt, curt
4 **a** snort; **b** spark; **c** hurt; **d** bark; **e** dark
6 trail, bail, fail, snail, jail, sail, tail, mail, quail; spoil, boil, coil, broil, foil, toil, soil, oil
7 scoot, boot, toot, shoot, loot, root, hoot; tweet, beet, feet, sweet, meet, fleet, sleet, greet, sheet
9 **a** trail; **b** snail; **c** feet; **d** oil; **e** meet; **f** sail